RECORDS FOREVER

RECORDS FOREVER

HOCKEY'S UNBEATABLE ACHIEVEMENTS

ANDREW PODNIEKS

FENN

M & S

Library and Archives Canada Cataloguing in Publication

Podnieks, Andrew
    NHL records forever : hockey's unbeatable achievements / Andrew Podnieks.

ISBN 978-0-7710-5103-6

    1. National Hockey League—Miscellanea.
2. Hockey—Records. 3. Hockey—Miscellanea. I. Title.

GV847.8.N3P6 2011   796.962'64   C2011-905240-7

We acknowledge the financial support of the Government of Canada through the Book Publishing Industry Development Program and that of the Government of Ontario through the Ontario
Media Development Corporation's Ontario Book Initiative. We further acknowledge the support
of the Canada Council for the Arts and the Ontario Arts Council for our publishing program.

Published simultaneously in the United States of America by McClelland & Stewart Ltd., P.O.
Box 1030, Plattsburgh, New York 12901

Library of Congress Control Number: 2011935924

Printed and bound in the United States of America

Fenn/McClelland & Stewart Ltd.
75 Sherbourne Street
Toronto, Ontario
M5A 2P9
www.mcclelland.com

1   2   3   4   5   14   13   12   11

CONTENTS

UNBEATABLE GAME RECORDS

INTRODUCTION

WHEN IT COMES TO SPORTS, there is no truer saying than records are meant to be broken. That, after all, is the Olympic ideal conveyed by its mandate of faster, higher, stronger (citius, altius, fortius, for the Latinphile). Yet, while every generation tries to improve on the previous one, there are some records that defy time and age, defy athletes of this era and the next and many more to come. In baseball, it might be Joe DiMaggio's fifty-six-game hitting streak. The NFL has Brett Favre's streak of consecutive games. In golf, it seems impossible that any player could win a major by fifteen strokes again, as Tiger Woods did at the U.S. Open at Pebble Beach in 2000.

Hockey has its own incredible records, and while many have or will be broken this year or next, there is a core group that will never be broken. Never? Never! Of course, never is a long time, as they saying goes, but some records that are celebrated in this book were set decades ago, and in succeeding years no Orr or Howe or Gretzky or Lemieux beat them, so how could any great player of the future?

Records come in various shapes and sizes. In hockey, they can easily be grouped into records by game, by season, and by career. That's how the records in this book have been divided, so that when one considers a record in one category it isn't being compared like apples to oranges with a record from another category.

Each of the three groups has a distinct character to it. A game record, for instance, might seem unbelievable, but it is, in some respect, the easiest to set because it is but a blip on the screen. Even scoring ten points in a game, as Darryl Sittler famously did in 1976, is the result of

one magical night. It's a record that won't be beat, but it can't be compared to Wayne Gretzky scoring nearly 2,900 points over 1,400 games and twenty years. So, game records are the result of a remarkable, but quick, spark-of-genius performance.

A season-long record is remarkable because it takes some eighty-two games and many months to achieve. There is no fluky aspect to this, at least not entirely, but sometimes such a record is the result of a player or team going on a hot streak and not letting up, but it's a streak that cannot be repeated all the same. Consider that in 1979–80, the Philadelphia Flyers went thirty-five games without a loss, a record that hasn't come close to being matched before or since. Yet the Flyers didn't even win the Cup that year. But for a stretch, they got hot and rode that streak for an incredibly long time. When their "Awakenings" moment was over, they returned to being a normally excellent team.

Of course, the most impressive records are those achieved over a career. These are the ones that define greatness, and only the best of the best can ever hope to achieve these. Doing something for one night is well within the realm of possibility; for a season, reasonable; but a career? These are the records that speak the loudest and are the toughest to beat. Who can possibly come close to Martin Brodeur's (ongoing) record of regular-season shutouts? To match him defies logic and would redefine the meaning of being consistently great. And therein lies the definition of career records, that combination of being consistent and being great—performance plus time equals immortality.

Taken as a group, the fifty records in this book are a way of understanding the long and storied history of the NHL. The records are achieved by hall of famers and the relatively obscure, by oldtimers and active players. They are set in two seconds and thirty-two years and every conceivable timeframe in between. They are, each one, incredible, and, for one reason or another, they are unmatchable.

Andrew Podnieks
Toronto, August 2011

UNBEATABLE
CAREER
RECORDS

RED HORNER: PUGNACIOUS SUPERSTAR

THE RECORD Toronto Maple Leafs defenceman Red Horner, the "bad boy" of his era, led the NHL in penalty minutes five seasons in a row, from 1932–33 to 1936–37. In all, he was PIMs king seven times.

HOW IT WAS DONE Reginald "Red" Horner was a large defenceman who anchored the Leafs' blue-line for twelve years. One of the most feared players of his day—skilled as well as tough—he never turned down an invitation or an opportunity to fight. What Toronto owner and general manager Conn Smythe also liked about him was that he seldom put his team at a disadvantage because of his rough play. Horner went to the penalty box a lot, but he usually took someone with him. And his pugnacious play went hand-in-hand with the Leafs winning. While he led the league in PIMs for seven of eight years, the Leafs went to the Stanley Cup Final five times. Horner epitomized the team's style of play, one founded on Smythe's famous mantra, "If you can't beat 'em in the alley, you can't beat 'em on the ice."

The only time in an eight-year period that Horner didn't lead the league in penalty minutes was 1937–38 when Art Coulter had ninety to Horner's eighty-two. When he retired in 1940, Horner had 1,254

PIERRE PILOTE (LEFT) RECEIVES THE NORRIS TROPHY.

HALL OF FAMERS Being a goon and fighting a lot is one thing, but being a tough guy as well as a superstar is another thing altogether. Horner is an inductee of the Hockey Hall of Fame (1965), but it has been fully half a century since a player has been both a penalty king and future HHOFer. The last was Pierre Pilote, who led the NHL with 165 PIMs in 1960–61 and went on to be inducted. Before that, there were another eleven besides Horner and Pilote who could claim the glory of being a Hall of Famer and the grit of being a feared fighter—Joe Hall, Sprague Cleghorn, Georges Boucher, Reg Noble, Nels Stewart, Eddie Shore, Red Dutton, Art Coulter, Jack Stewart, Maurice Richard, and Ted Lindsay. This clearly shows that in the old days, the best fighters were top stars and vice versa. But in the modern era, a scorer scores and a fighter fights, and never shall the twain meet.

THE INFAMOUS

The height of the fighting days spanned from the Boston and Philadelphia teams of the 1970s through to the Oilers of the early 1980s. Yet through all this time, the only person to lead the league in PIMs even three years in a row was Dave Schultz, who was penalty king from 1972–75. "The Hammer" also led the league again in 1977–78. Gus Mortson is the only other player to lead the league in penalty minutes four times, but he never achieved this dubious feat even twice in a row. Tiger Williams, the career leader in penalty minutes by a wide margin, led the league in PIMs three times, never consecutively.

career penalty minutes, tops on the all-time list. Horner set the season record for penalty minutes in 1935–36 when he had 167 minutes, breaking Eddie Shore's record by just two minutes (or, one minor penalty).

There are several reasons why the totals seem low by today's standards. First, this was an era of a forty-eight-game schedule. Second, the tabulation of penalty minutes was different; today, a game misconduct is automatically counted as ten minutes, not so in the 1930s. And lastly, players were seldom given misconducts or game misconducts, no matter how brazen their behaviour. New NHL rules got much gratuitous fighting out of the game through harsher penalties, but in Horner's era brawls were common and players generally got off with five minutes for being the main combatant and two for just about anything else. If Horner played today, his PIM totals would have been substantially higher.

WHY IT WON'T BE EQUALLED Hockey has gone through decades of melees and bench-clearing brawls to get to where it is today, an infinitely more civilized game based on speed and skill more than intimidation. In the thirties, all players were expected to fight as well as contribute skill to the

TORONTO MAPLE LEAFS ™

Nine players have amassed more than 3,000 penalty minutes during their careers, but no one is likely ever to catch Dave "Tiger" Williams. His 3,966 penalty minutes has been the record since he retired in 1988, and no one since has come particularly close to catching him. Second is Dale Hunter with 3,563, and third is Tie Domi with 3,515. Given that 300 penalty minutes is a lot for any one year (Zenon Konopka led the way in 2010–11 with 307—he also led the league the previous year with 265 minutes), a player would have to hit this mark for thirteen years to catch Tiger. Sitting in twelfth on the all-time list is Chris Chelios with 2,891, and once he is inducted into the Hockey Hall of Fame he will have the distinction of being the most penalized member of all inductees.

team. Starting in the 1960s, teams employed a designated fighter, a player who got ice time merely to intimidate and fight the opposition. That didn't change much until recently.

Teams today have no roster spot available for a player whose one and only attribute is fighting, so in that respect today's game is more akin to the game of Horner's day. Fighting continues to be a part of hockey, but it is practised by players who possess at least a modicum of skating, checking, or scoring ability. Today, skill players seldom drop their gloves; it's too risky and dangerous, and it's not conducive to winning hockey games to have a player risk a lengthy penalty just to fight.

"BOOM BOOM" PLAYS FIFTY-THREE STRAIGHT STANLEY CUP FINAL GAMES

THE RECORD Between 1951 and 1960 there were a total of fifty-three games played in the Stanley Cup Final. Only one player appeared in every game, Montreal's Bernie "Boom Boom" Geoffrion.

HOW IT WAS DONE Starting in 1951, the Montreal Canadiens appeared in the Stanley Cup Final for ten consecutive years, winning six times. It wasn't until 1961, when Chicago knocked off the Habs in six games, that Montreal was not one of the two teams advance to the Final. Of course, you have to be good to be lucky and lucky to be good, and Bernie Geoffrion was both.

The 1950–51 season was his first in the NHL, and he quickly turned into a scoring star to rival teammate Maurice Richard. He appeared in only eighteen regular-season games in his rookie season but dressed for all eleven playoff contests. In the coming years, "Boom Boom" missed many games during the regular season but always managed to glue his body back together for the post-season. In the two-year period 1956–58, he played only 83 of 140 games during the season but never missed a playoff game.

Part luck, the record also speaks to his incredible ability to endure pain and his super-human perseverance. Had the Bill Masterton Trophy been

RECORDS FOREVER

available in his day, he would surely have won it two or three times. He also might have increased his total by a few games in 1960, but the Habs were a perfect 8–0 in the playoffs, winning the Cup in the fewest games possible.

WHY IT WON'T BE EQUALLED

The quick and simple explanation is obvious. With thirty teams, all highly competitive, there is no way in the world any team will ever make it to the Stanley Cup Final ten straight years. Never. Ever. The only team even remotely close to this achievement since the Habs of the 1950s was the New York Islanders, appearing in five straight finals, 1980–84. Total consecutive finals games? A mere twenty-four.

BOOM BOOM'S CLOSE CALL

During practise one day in 1958, Geoffrion collided with a teammate. Moments after the seemingly innocuous contact he collapsed and was rushed to hospital where he underwent emergency surgery for a ruptured bowel. Doctors told him his season was over and possibly his career as well. Six weeks later, Geoffrion was in the lineup, helping the Habs to another Stanley Cup victory.

GREAT SCORER—BUT AT A PRICE

Geoffrion is the only NHLer to win the Art Ross Trophy and feel utter scorn and wrath—indeed, hatred is not too strong a word—from his own fans. In 1954–55, he had thirty-eight goals and seventy-five points, tops in the league by the end of the regular season. Near the end of the year, he and teammate Maurice Richard were neck-and-neck in the points race when the Rocket was suspended for the rest of the season for his assault on a linesman during a game. Geoffrion went on to outpace Richard by a single point during the final home game of the season to overtake the beloved Rocket and win the scoring race.

This was as close as Richard ever got to winning the Art Ross, and Geoffrion was booed mercilessly for his goal and two assists in the first period of a 4–2 win over the Rangers on Saturday night to overtake Richard in the points race. The next night, Geoffrion was held pointless in a 6–0 road loss to Detroit, but the "damage" had been done. He led the league in points—and robbed the more beloved "Rocket" of the glory.

UNBEATABLE CAREER RECORDS

FIFTY IN SIXTY-FOUR

Geoffrion became only the second NHLer to score fifty goals in a season, a feat he accomplished in 1960–61. The first player to reach the milestone was Maurice Richard, who got his fifty goals in just fifty games in 1944–45, a time when the league was watered down because of the departure of so many top players to war service. "Boom Boom," however, needed sixty-four games to reach the half century mark, but when he did, on March 16, 1961, he received a great ovation from the Forum fans during the team's 5–2 win over the Leafs.

The game pitted the top scorers in the league against each other, as Toronto's Frank Mahovlich was one goal back from "Boom Boom" with forty-eight, but the Big M was shut out the rest of the year and finished with that number. Geoffrion didn't add to his total after that night either, staying at fifty, even though there were still two games left in the season.

BERNIE GEOFFRION (#5) HUGS MAURICE RICHARD AFTER A MONTREAL GOAL.

GEOFFRION KISSES HIS FIFTIETH GOAL PUCK ON MARCH 16, 1961.

THE HABS WIN FIVE IN A ROW

THE RECORD It's a simply stated record: The Montreal Canadiens won the Stanley Cup five years in a row (1955–60). It's a feat that will never be equaled.

HOW IT WAS DONE After losing the 1947 Stanley Cup to Toronto, the Habs didn't make it to the Final again for three years. After that brief drought, the Stanley Cup Final was their domain for a decade. They won the Cup in 1953, but lost to the dynastic Red Wings in 1952, 1954, and 1955. In 1956, they vanquished the Wings in five games, beginning an unprecedented run of five straight wins. After beating Detroit, Montreal beat Boston the next two years, and then beat Toronto in 1959 and 1960.

Montreal and Detroit were the dominant teams of the 1950s. Between 1948 and 1955, the Red Wings won the league's regular-season title seven straight years, and on five of those occasions the Canadiens finished in second place.

But starting with the 1955–56 season, the Habs were simply unbeatable. They finished first overall by a colossal margin, winning forty-five of seventy games and amassing 100 points, the first time they

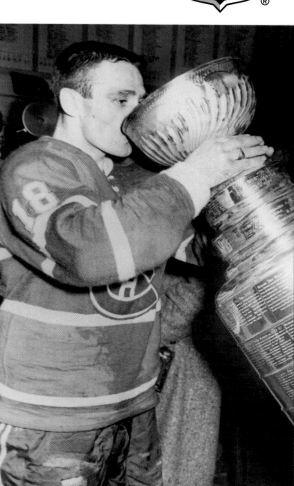

ISLANDERS DYNASTY ENDS

While the Islanders were the last team to make it to five straight Stanley Cup Finals, their last appearance, after four straight wins, was anti-climactic. They lost without much of a fight to an Edmonton team loaded with talent, ambition, and its own sense of history. The Islanders won game two by a convincing 6–1 score after the Oilers won the opener in uncharacteristic style, 1–0. But the final three games were all Gretzky and Company, as Edmonton outscored New York 19–6 to start a dynasty of its own.

ISLANDERS DEFENCEMAN DENIS POTVIN (LEFT) CONGRATULATES EDMONTON'S WAYNE GRETZKY AFTER THE 1984 CUP FINAL.

reached the century mark (Detroit, the only other team to have done so, had 100 twice). The Red Wings were way back in second place with seventy-six points. In the playoffs, the Habs weren't seriously challenged, winning the semi-finals against the Rangers in five games and needing only another five to finish off Detroit in the Final.

In 1956–57, the Habs finished second to the Red Wings, but while Montreal knocked off the Rangers again in a five-game semi-final, the Bruins upset Detroit in five games to advance to the Cup Final. The result was the same, though, a five-game win by Montreal. In 1957–58, the Habs were again on top in the regular season and crushed Detroit in four straight to get to another Stanley Cup Final against Boston. This was the one moment in the streak when the Habs might have been had. Teams split the first four games and the fifth went to overtime, but Maurice Richard scored at 5:45 of the fourth period to give Montreal a 3–2 win in the game and 3–2 lead in the series. The Habs closed out the Cup triumph three nights later with a 5–3 win at the Garden in Boston.

The next year, Montreal beat Chicago in six games, none of which went to overtime, and then clinched Cup number four with a five-game win over the Leafs, who had got to the playoffs with a miracle finish to the regular season. In 1959–60, Montreal had

RECORDS FOREVER

its most dominant playoff run to win its record fifth Stanley Cup win in a row, whipping the Hawks in four straight and outscoring them 14–6, and doing the same to the Leafs, winning four straight by a cumulative score of 15–5.

WHY IT WON'T BE EQUALLED In this day and age, making it to the Stanley Cup Final in consecutive years is a miracle. Winning twice in a row is unheard of, the last team to do so being the Red Wings in 1997 and 1998, and winning even three in a row was last done by the Islanders when they won four in a row (1980–83). With thirty teams, a salary cap, and parity ensuring no team either falls too low or rises too high for too long, the very concept of a dynasty is long over.

SIX IN A ROW?

The Canadiens had a great chance to begin their dynasty a year earlier when they faced Detroit in a best-of-seven Final. As it turned out, Detroit's home-ice advantage was the key to victory as every game was won by the home side. In game seven, at the Olympia in Detroit, the Red Wings stormed out to a 2–0 lead in the second period after a scoreless opening twenty minutes, and they added a third goal early in the final period before Montreal scored once to make it a 3–1 game. The Red Wings won for the fourth time in six years, their greatest success in franchise history, and the start of the Canadiens dynasty was delayed a year.

CLOSE CALLS Poor Steve Smith will forever go down in history as the player who likely prevented the Edmonton Oilers from winning five in a row in the 1980s. The Oil won in 1984 and 1985, and had just as strong a team in 1986, but Smith made an historic gaffe in game seven of their second-round series against Calgary. Midway through the third period, with the score tied, 2–2, Smith made a terrible pass through his own crease that banked off goalie Grant Fuhr's skate and into his own goal. The Flames won the game and series, and went to the Cup Final before losing to the Habs. The Oilers, meanwhile, won the Cup again in 1987 and 1988. But for that pass, Edmonton might well have won five in a row.

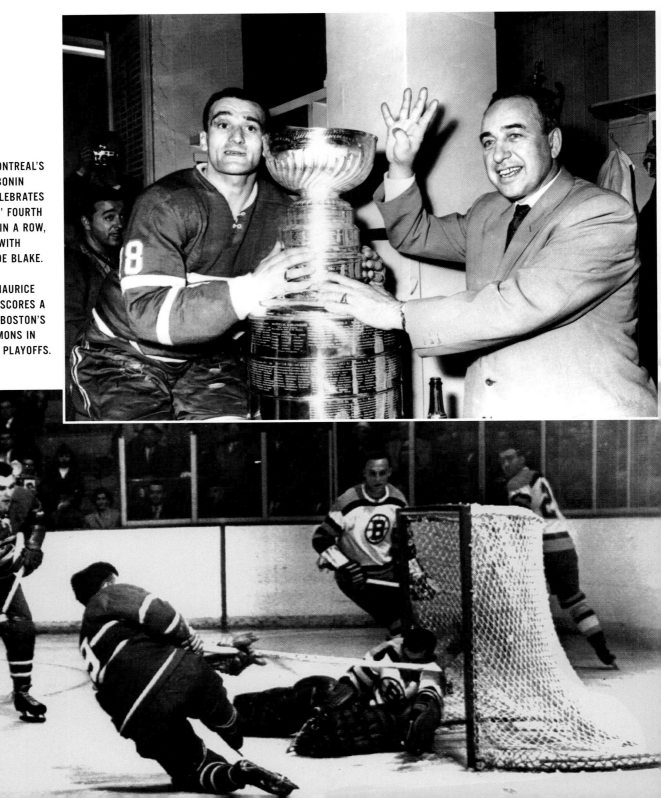

RIGHT: MONTREAL'S MARCEL BONIN (LEFT) CELEBRATES THE HABS' FOURTH CUP WIN IN A ROW, IN 1959, WITH COACH TOE BLAKE.

BELOW: MAURICE RICHARD SCORES A GOAL ON BOSTON'S DON SIMMONS IN THE 1957 PLAYOFFS.

GLENN HALL STARTS 502 STRAIGHT GAMES

THE RECORD From the first game of Detroit's 1955–56 season, October 6, 1955, until November 7, 1962, a period of more than seven years, exactly 502 games, and more than 30,000 minutes of game action, goalie Glenn Hall played every minute of every regular season game, first with the Red Wings and then with Chicago.

HOW IT WAS DONE If a team's general manager trades Terry Sawchuk because he feels he has a better goalie, he had better be right. Jack Adams, GM of Detroit, did just that in the summer of 1955 because he believed twenty-four-year-old Glenn Hall was better. Hall played every game for the Red Wings for the following two years—140 straight games. Adams then traded Hall and Ted Lindsay to Chicago for Jerry Wilson, Forbes Kennedy, Bill Preston, and goalie Hank Bassen.

Hall continued to play every game for the next five years, finally missing one thirteen games into the 1962–63 season—his 503rd straight start—when he pulled himself midway through the first period because of back pains. That game, against Boston on November 7, 1962, ended in a 3–3 tie. Hall had suffered a pinched nerve in his back the previous day in practice, but he tried to play anyway given the magnitude of his streak.

FULL SEASONS In Original Six days and earlier, it was perfectly common for a goalie to play every minute of every game, but as the schedule expanded to forty-eight games, then fifty, sixty, and seventy, those efforts were far fewer. To put Hall's record in perspective, he played seven full seasons in a row. The next closest was Terry Sawchuk who played every minute for TWO seasons! Some goalies might play seventy games, but not 4,200 minutes. Many of the greatest goalies of the era played a full season, but that's it—Johnny Bower, Roger Crozier, Eddie Johnston, Harry Lumley, Jimmy McNeil, Jacques Plante, Gump Worsley. Crozier was the last to play seventy games, but he played only 4,168 minutes in 1964–65 with Detroit, being replaced on two occasions by backup Carl Wetzel.

HALL'S OTHER DISTINCTIONS
Glenn Hall's only Stanley Cup win came with Chicago in 1961, but he won the Vezina Trophy three times, first in 1962–63, again in 1966–67 (with Denis DeJordy), and finally, and most improbably, with Jacques Plante when the tandem backstopped the expansion St. Louis Blues in 1968–69. Hall was thirty-eight by this point. He was also the number-one goalie for the Blues in their inaugural season (1967–68), and although they were swept by Montreal in the Final, Hall was named winner of the Conn Smythe Trophy, the only expansion player to be so honoured in the first decade of the trophy's existence.

Hall faced only one shot in the game, and that came at 10:21 when he surrendered a goal to Murray Oliver. At that point, Hall skated off the ice and to the dressing room, and the game was delayed several minutes as Denis DeJordy came out of the stands to put his equipment on. Hall had been too proud to allow the new goalie the start, despite the pains in his back at practice the day before. Regardless, DeJordy played the remaining 49:39 of the game. He had been recalled from the Buffalo Bisons and was considered the best goalie not in the NHL. The game ended 3–3, but Hall's consecutive minutes streak was over.

WHY IT WON'T BE EQUALLED

An eighty-two-game season. Coaches who need two quality goalies. Thirty teams spread across North America travelling by plane. Increased competition, harder shots, more demanding schedules. These are the main reasons why Glenn Hall's record is, without question, the most bullet proof record that will never—can never—be broken. What's most amazing of all, though, is that Hall played every minute of every game. Starting 502 in a row is incredible enough, but imagine never getting pulled, never playing so badly, or getting hurt, so that the coach has to resort to his backup!

GRANT FUHR OF ST. LOUIS.

MOST GAMES IN A SEASON
One record that was impossible for Hall to maintain was most games played in a season. As the NHL expanded, so did the schedule, and as the pressure to win grew, coaches were often more inclined to ride one goalie as long as possible. In the modern era of the (briefly) eighty-four-game schedule and now longstanding eighty-two-game schedule, several goalies have played seventy-seven games in a season. The record, however, belongs to Grant Fuhr, who played seventy-nine of eighty-two games for St. Louis in 1995–96. As unbelievable, that included a streak of seventy-six consecutive starts. Not only is this an incredible amount of play, it is a record for which the coach must take some credit. In this case, that's Mike Keenan. Keenan being Keenan, though, he was not averse to pulling and changing his goalies frequently, and although Fuhr played in seventy-nine games, he was replaced more than a dozen times.

ROBBIE IRONS' CAREER LASTS THREE MINUTES, ONE SECOND

THE RECORD On November 13, 1968, goalie Robbie Irons played three minutes and one second of a game for St. Louis against the New York Rangers. It turned out to be the only time he ever played in the NHL, making this the shortest goalie career in NHL history.

HOW IT WAS DONE You can thank Scotty Bowman for this one, in some respects. Bowman had convinced goalie Jacques Plante to come out of retirement in June of 1968. Plante acquiesced because his wife's health was much improved—the main reason he had retired in the first place—and because the coach promised to rotate Plante with another all-time great, Glenn Hall. Plante, at thirty-nine, had no interest in either starting every game or sitting on the bench as backup.

Bowman's plan was different. He'd rotate Hall and Plante, and when each wasn't playing the other would be in the press box, in street clothes, with not a worry in the world. "Every time you get on the bench, you're all keyed up and tense," Plante admitted. "Sitting in the stands and knowing you have the day off is a wonderful feeling." Of course, the coach and his two goalies knew that each goalie would play sixty minutes of every game, so when Bowman dressed a rookie as his backup, he knew there was no danger

THE CRUELEST CUT

Everyone can understand how one-game wonders happen— a player is recalled because of injury, or as a goodwill gesture by the team, or as a test to see how the player fares at the highest level. But of those 300-plus players in this category, there are some who recorded an assist or goal—and never played again! One would think if a player scored in his first NHL game he'd at least merit a second game, just to see if he can keep this pace up. But, no, that sometimes doesn't happen. Players who have a goal in their one and only NHL game include: Brad Fast (2003–04, with Carolina), Rollie Huard (1930–31, Toronto), Dean Morton (1989–90, Detroit), and Raymie Skilton (1917–18, Montreal Wanderers). Another sixteen players earned an assist in their one and only NHL game.

because hell and high water would have to arrive before he would take out either star goalie for an inexperienced backup. Plante and Hall were, simply, the best of the best.

But on the night of November 13, 1968, something happened that no one could have anticipated. The sequence of events started just 1:16 into the game when Vic Hadfield of the Rangers beat Hall with a long shot, an embarrassing

CLOSE, BUT... Christian Soucy made his NHL debut in goal for Chicago on March 31, 1994. He replaced Jeff Hackett at 16:39 of the first period after Hackett had allowed three goals to Washington. "The team needed a jump at that time," said assistant coach Paul Baxter. "Certainly, it [the goalie change] got their attention." Soucy, an undrafted goalie from Gatineau, Quebec, had played two years at the University of Vermont before turning pro with the Indianapolis Ice of the IHL at the start of this 1993–94 season.

How could Soucy realize when he played that 3:21 to end the first period that coach Darryl Sutter would bring Hackett back to start the second and play him the rest of the game? And how could Soucy know then he would never again play in the NHL? But that's what happened. Hackett went the rest of the way, the Hawks lost, 6–3, and Soucy was soon back in the minors with Indianapolis. He played another decade in the "I," then in the CHL, ECHL, AHL, WCHL, and UHL—but never again in the NHL.

At least he retired with a 0.00 goals-against average. Not many goalies can say that.

goal for Hall to give up. Just a few seconds later, Blues teammate Robert Picard was called for a penalty by referee Vern Buffey, which further incensed Hall. Making matters worse, Hall was wearing a mask for the first time and was obviously feeling a bit uncomfortable. Ten seconds into the Rangers' power play, there was a whistle and Buffey skated in front of Hall's crease. The goalie started a heated argument, which ended with Hall cuffing the referee with his catcher's glove, earning an automatic ten-minute misconduct and a game misconduct.

The game misconduct was the first of Hall's illustrious career. Bowman had to put Irons into the net for what turned out to be three minutes and one second of game action while Plante hurried down from the press box and got dressed. He went into the game and Irons back to the end of the bench, and the Blues rallied for a 3–1 win. Irons? He never played in the NHL again.

WHY IT WON'T BE EQUALLED

In hockey's early days, it was not uncommon for a starter to be sick or injured and need to be replaced at the last minute by a goalie in the stands, but in these instances the rookie goalie at least played the full game or the rest of the game. Of course, there have also been many instances of a goalie coming in unexpectedly for a shorter period of time, but there has always been some length to the emergency appearance. Furthermore, any backup goalie in such a case is usually the team's regular backup and will play at least several games during any season. What is peculiar about Irons' situation is that he was actually a sub

ONE-GAME WONDERS

There are more than 300 players who have made but a single appearance in the NHL, and the strange thing is you never know when one game will turn into a thousand or turn out to be the one and only. In 2010–11, for instance, some fourteen players appeared in their first and only NHL game to date— Adam Henrique (New Jersey), Rob Klinkhammer (Chicago), Paul Postma (Atlanta), Carl Klingberg (Atlanta), Joe Colborne (Toronto), Matt Campanale (Islanders), Brandon Pirri (Chicago), Shane Sims (Islanders), Evan Brophey (Chicago), Matt Frattin (Toronto), Brodie Dupont (Rangers), Jamie Arniel (Boston), Jamie Doornbosch (Islanders), and Colton Sceviour (Dallas). How many of these will become full-time NHLers—and how many will never play again? There's no way of knowing until you look back at their records years later. The only one of the group to record a point was Colborne, who had an assist.

GLENN HALL.

for the backup who was subbing for the starter who was tossed from a game after only 2:01 of game action.

Irons, who was six days shy of his twenty-second birthday on the night in question, was an excellent prospect. He had started in the New York Rangers system, playing junior for the Kitchener Rangers, but the Blues acquired him in the summer of 1968 in a significant deal, along with Camille Henry and Bill Plager, for Wayne Rivers and Don Caley. But coach Scotty Bowman had Glenn Hall and Jacques Plante as his two goalies, arguably the two greatest puck stoppers of all time. Irons wasn't needed.

Nonetheless, Irons had a fourteen-year career in the minors, an excellent one at that, but he never got another chance to play in the NHL. In fact, his number 30 sweater was retired by the Fort Wayne Comets, the team for whom he played the vast majority of his career in the IHL. By sheer dint of the tens of thousands of NHL games and goalie appearances and such a short career never happening before or since, one has to believe it will never happen again.

THE BRIEFEST APPEARANCE POSSIBLE

The 2010 World Championship came to a crashing end for Sweden in the semi-finals. Leading the Czech Republic, 2–1, for half the game, Tre Kronor allowed Karel Rachunek to tie the score with less than eight seconds left in regulation. The Czechs then won in a shootout, sending Sweden to the bronze-medal game against Germany. That was an easier game and opponent for the Swedes. They were comfortably winning the game, 2–1, when a bizarre twist occurred near game's end. German coach Uwe Krupp pulled his goalie to try to tie the game, and Jonas Andersson scored into the empty net to make it 3–1 for the Swedes. In the dying seconds, the Swedes were called for icing. There was exactly one second left on the clock, but the officials had to have a faceoff in the Sweden end to complete the game.

After the icing, Tre Kronor coach Bengt-Ake Gustafsson called a timeout, a silly action given his team's two-goal lead and a single second on the clock. During the stoppage, he pulled goalie Jonas Gustavsson and inserted twenty-two-year-old Anders Lindback. Lindback merely stood in the crease, the linesman dropped the puck, and the game ended. This was Lindback's first—and still only—"appearance" with the Swedish national team, and might go down in history as the shortest career in hockey history—one second.

"ELBOWS" IN TOP-TEN SCORING FOR TWENTY-ONE CONSECUTIVE YEARS

THE RECORD From 1949–50 to 1969–70, Gordie Howe finished among the top ten scoring leaders every year, a record of consistency twenty-one years long that will never be equaled.

HOW IT WAS DONE Gordie Howe's first NHL season was 1946–47. He scored just seven goals and had twenty-two points in fifty-eight games, but by his fourth year he had thirty-five goals and sixty-eight points playing on a line with best friend Ted Lindsay and veteran Sid Abel, the troika becoming known as the Production Line for their incredible offence. In 1949–50, they finished 1–2–3 in league scoring, Lindsay with seventy-eight points followed by Abel with sixty-nine and Howe with his sixty-eight. The team finished first in the regular season and went on to win the Stanley Cup. A dynasty was born.

In each of the next four years, Howe was the top scorer and Art Ross Trophy winner by a wide margin. He won the scoring title by margins of twenty, seventeen, twenty-four, and fourteen points, and in an era when the top point getter had around eighty-five points, this margin represented about 25 per cent. Howe finished in fifth place in 1954–55, usurped by young Bernie Geoffrion and Jean Beliveau as well

SMYTHE'S DICTUM APPLIED TO HOWE

Toronto owner Conn Smythe once said he didn't like players who looked bad in a loss or players who looked good in a loss. And he didn't like players who looked bad in a win. What he liked were players who looked good in a win because they were the ones who drove the team's success. Well, during Howe's run of twenty-one seasons in the top ten, the Red Wings won the Stanley Cup four times, went to the Cup Final five times, and missed the playoffs five times. Keeping in mind that Howe was a superstar for two—or, arguably, three—generations of players, it's a remarkable testament to his being part of the team's success, both in his twenties and thirties—and his forties.

as veterans Maurice Richard and Dutch Reibel. But while a new generation of stars entered the league, Howe just kept rolling along, helping the Red Wings reach the playoffs year after year and scoring his share of the goals.

Howe won the scoring title in 1956–57, for the first time in four years, but this time his margin was just four points over Lindsay. Perhaps his most incredible season was 1962–63. He won the Art Ross Trophy again with eighty-six points, but every other player in the top ten wasn't even in the NHL when he started his career seventeen years earlier. He had eighty-six points while Andy Bathgate, whose rookie season was 1952–53, was second with eighty-one. Third was Stan Mikita (rookie in 1958–59), and fourth Frank Mahovlich (rookie 1956–57). Fifth was Henri Richard (rookie

1955–56), sixth was Jean Beliveau (1950–51), seventh Johnny Bucyk (1955–56), eighth Alex Delvecchio (1950–51), and tied for ninth were Bobby Hull (1957–58) and Murray Oliver (1957–58). This was to be Howe's last Art Ross Trophy, but he remained in the top ten for the rest of the decade. Incredibly, he had his only 100-point season in 1968–69 when he had 103 and finished third behind Hull (107) and Phil Esposito (126). Howe was a day shy of his forty-first birthday.

THE GREATS

Howe's is a record for the best of the best, so a look at other hall of famers is revealing. Phil Esposito stayed in the top ten for eight straight years (1967–75). Guy Lafleur managed just six years (1974–80), and Marcel Dionne five years (1978–83). Because of injury, Mario Lemieux managed only five (1985–90). Howe's teammate Ted Lindsay managed seven in a row (1947–54), and Jean Beliveau also had seven (1954–61). The only player who comes remotely close to Howe's twenty-one straight years was Wayne Gretzky, who placed in the top ten for thirteen straight years (1979–92). But even the Great One didn't stay as consistently great for as long as Mr. Hockey.

WHY IT WON'T BE EQUALLED In order to match Howe's record, a player must defy the odds in several ways. First, he simply has to play in the NHL for twenty straight seasons. In ninety-five years of NHL play and more than 7,000 players, exactly fifty-six have managed to stick around for twenty seasons. Next, a player has to remain injury free during those two decades. If he misses too many games in any one year, he won't make it into the top ten. Then, of course, he has to be consistent over an extraordinary period of time. Putting all these elements together, Howe's streak is simply unmatchable.

HOWE'S YEAR BY YEAR Here is Howe's finish in the scoring race during his twenty-one-year run: 3rd, 1st, 1st, 1st, 1st, 5th, 2nd, 1st, 4th, 4th, T-5th, 5th, T-3rd, 1st, 5th, 3rd, 5th, T-4th, 3rd, 3rd, 9th. Incredibly, he played the complete season in sixteen of these twenty-one seasons and never missed more than six games in any other year. Howe also scored at least twenty-three goals for twenty-two successive seasons, another record never to be bettered.

RECORDS FOREVER

NUMBER 4 OWNS THE NORRIS

THE RECORD Between 1967–68 and 1974–75, Bobby Orr won the Norris Trophy as the league's best defenceman every year.

HOW IT WAS DONE When Harry Howell accepted the Norris Trophy playing for the New York Rangers in 1966–67, he thanked the league for honouring him and noted that no one else but Orr was going to win it for a very long time. How right he was. After Orr's rookie campaign, he won the trophy every full season he played, eight consecutive years, losing out only when knee injuries began to slow his career in 1975-76 (Denis Potvin won that year). He was great on offence, great in his own end, tough as nails, and played on a dominating team. What more could one ask for when dishing out an award for the league's best defenceman?

In Orr's first four years, he took the team from last place to the Stanley Cup. He went from forty-one points as a rookie to 120, winning the Art Ross Trophy over teammate Phil Esposito by a whopping twenty-one points. It has been said a million times before, but Orr simply re-invented the position of defence. He loved rushing the puck up ice from behind his own goal right to the crease of his opponent's net. If he didn't take the puck himself, he would happily pass

BRAD PARK.

off and head up ice without the puck, creating havoc for the defending team which now had to contend with four rushing players, not three. And because Orr was gambling, he didn't skate to the corner—he went to the net. His sole objective was to score or create scoring chances. And, if he lost the puck or the other team made the transition from defence to offence quickly, there was no one in the league who could skate back as quickly as number 4.

In his rookie season he had 102 penalty minutes, testament to opponent's trying to intimidate him, and equal testament to his unwillingness to back down. After year one, he was also known as one of the toughest players in the game. For eight years, while he was healthy, no one played the game like him, and no blue-liner was as dominant all over the ice as Orr.

WHY IT WON'T BE EQUALLED

The only other NHLer to win eight individual trophies consecutively was Wayne Gretzky, who was awarded the Hart Trophy every year from 1980 to 1987. To be such a great player at the highest level and with such consistency, for so long, is rare. To earn the admiration of friends and foes for such a length is rarer. Perhaps some defenceman will come along to eclipse Orr, but if Doug Harvey, Paul Coffey, and Nicklas Lidstrom are unable to create a more lasting memory than Orr, who knows when such a player will?

THE DEATH OF THE RUSHING DEFENCEMAN Orr's greatest assets were his skating and his determination to take the puck to the other team's goal. Many great defencemen before and since have moved the puck fluidly out of their own zone, and sometimes into the opponent's end, but few continued on, trying to make moves to get right to the goal. Defencemen today are too worried about being caught out of position, or they aren't skilled enough with the puck to get to the net. They cross the blue-line, curl, and try to dish the puck off rather than go full steam to the net trying to score or draw a penalty. Yes, Orr changed the game, but with time the game has, unfortunately, changed right back.

HARRY HOWELL OF THE RANGERS (RIGHT) WAS THE LAST DEFENCEMAN
TO WIN THE NORRIS TROPHY BEFORE ORR WON EIGHT IN A ROW.

THE "POCKET ROCKET" IS THE GREATEST WINNER

THE RECORD Henri Richard might not be as revered as his much older brother, Maurice, but Henri has won the Stanley Cup as a player eleven times—more than anyone else.

HOW IT WAS DONE Henri Richard was part of two dynasties, arriving on the scene at the right time and staying with a uniquely successful team for the full twenty years of his career. He won the Stanley Cup more often than not, starting in 1955. He joined the Montreal Canadiens that fall and was quickly named "Pocket Rocket" because he was the younger (by fifteen years)—and smaller—brother of the great Maurice "Rocket" Richard. He was also joining a team loaded with talent, and the Habs won the Cup for the next five years. Maurice retired after this dynasty, in 1960, but it didn't take long for the Habs to build another great team.

While Toronto got much of the national attention for winning three in a row—between 1962–64—and a fourth in the Centennial year of 1967, the Habs also won four Cups in the 1960s—1965 and 1966, and then again in 1968 and 1969. Henri wasn't just a passenger on these teams; he was a key element to the wins. In the 1966 Final against Detroit, he scored the Stanley Cup-winning goal at 2:20 of overtime of game six.

COACH TOE BLAKE HUGS HENRI RICHARD AFTER MONTREAL WON THE STANLEY CUP IN 1966.

Henri became the captain of the team in 1971, after Jean Beliveau retired. Henri scored another Cup-winner that year, making him one of only five players to have scored two Cup-winning goals (along with Jack Darragh, Bobby Orr, Jacques Lemaire, and Mike Bossy). As captain, Henri took the team to his final Stanley Cup triumph, in 1973. He retired early in the 1974–75 season when injuries had slowed him and decreased effectiveness.

WHY IT WON'T BE EQUALLED The only possible way to come close to this sheer volume of victory is to be part of two, if not three, dynasties. But, since the dynasty is, by the very nature of the new game, a dinosaur, it's difficult imagining a player winning even four or five Cups during his career anymore, let alone double or triple that number. As well, a player has to be good enough to be a star on a team full of stars (as any Cup team is) and be consistently good for two decades. If no team can win eleven Cups in a 15–20-year span any longer, no player can, either.

DETROIT'S STEVE YZERMAN WON THE CUP FOR THE FIRST TIME IN 1997.

RECORDS FOREVER

HENRI RICHARD WON THE CUP FOR THE ELEVENTH AND FINAL TIME IN 1973.

HENRI SPECIAL IN HIS OWN RIGHT

The younger Richard has always had to cope with being considered, by the general populace, the second best player in the family. No one talks about the "fire in his eyes" the way they do Maurice, but in truth Henri had the greater statistical career in almost every way. Henri played twenty years; Maurice eighteen. Henri played 1,256 games; Maurice 978. Henri finished with 1,046 points; Maurice had 965. Henri won eleven Cups; Maurice eight. And yet, the only individual trophy Henri ever won was the Bill Masterton Trophy, in 1973–74. He was a First Team All-Star only once (Maurice was named eight times). Both, though, are in the Hockey Hall of Fame, and both left strong legacies in Montreal.

MONTREAL'S OTHER GREAT WINNERS   The key to any run of Cup success is the dynasty. Jean Beliveau won ten Cups in similar fashion to Henri, the only difference being the last one Henri won in 1973. The only player to win as many as eight Cups with a team other than Montreal was Red Kelly who won four with Detroit in the 1950s and four with Toronto in the 1960s. Again, two dynasties. Yvan Cournoyer also won ten, and Claude Provost won nine, not enough to get him into the Hall of Fame, though. Maurice Richard and Jacques Lemaire join Red Kelly with eight. In all, only seven players have won even eight Stanley Cup titles.

In the last forty-five years, since the major expansion of 1967, only Montreal has won more than five Cups, with ten victories. So even if a player dressed for the Canadiens from 1967 to 1993 (twenty-six years, or, the length of Gordie Howe's NHL career), he still would have fallen short of Henri Richard's record. Edmonton has won five Cups, Detroit and the Islanders have won the Cup four times, and three teams have won three championships—Colorado, Pittsburgh, and New Jersey.

GORDIE HOWE PLAYS IN TWENTY-THREE NHL ALL-STAR GAMES

THE RECORD On February 5, 1980, Gordie Howe played in his twenty-third NHL All-Star Game, at the new Joe Louis Arena in Detroit.

HOW IT WAS DONE For the first nineteen All-Star Games in which Howe played, the format featured the Stanley Cup champion of the previous year playing the best of the rest of the league. That meant for anyone to play in the game he had to have won the Cup or been considered one of the best players at his position. Howe was part of four Cup teams in Detroit, which meant he was selected to the team the other fifteen years by virtue of his on-ice performance.

The All-Star Game went to a full best-on-best format in 1969, and Howe was again selected in his last three NHL seasons before retiring, bringing his total to twenty-two. When he played in the NHL again in 1979–80 for one final season, coach Scotty Bowman added him to the Wales Conference side as a coach's pick. The ovation Howe received from the fans he knew so well will go down in the annals of the sport as the greatest in All-Star Game history.

The game was played before a then-record crowd of 21,002, and Howe came onto the ice with former teammates, the long retired Sid Abel and

GORDIE HOWE (MIDDLE) JOINS WAYNE GRETZKY (RIGHT) AT THE 1986 ALL-STAR GAME.

DETAILS OF THE GAME

Howe helped goalie Tony Esposito set a record for the shortest appearance by a goalie in All-Star Game history. In the old days, one goalie played the entire game, but on this night a wicked slapshot from Howe hurt Esposito's glove hand fifteen minutes into the game and he had to leave. Howe even managed to get on the score sheet, earning the only assist on Real Cloutier's late goal, giving the Wales a 6–3 win. Howe also played against Wayne Gretzky this night.

A SPECIAL TIME FOR GORDIE

The Olympia in Detroit was one of the great old Original Six buildings of the NHL, but it was replaced by the Joe Louis Arena early in the 1979–80 season. The Red Wings played their first game there on December 27, 1979, losing to St. Louis, 3–2. Howe's participation in the All-Star Game at the new arena had particular and nostalgic importance for him and the fans who had watched him play at the Olympia for twenty-five years. As well, the league held a banquet the night before the game at the Plaza Hotel. A record 1,500 guests watched as the old Production Line of Howe, Ted Lindsay, and Sid Abel were honoured.

Ted Lindsay, who were dressed nicely in suits and looking like the fine elder gentlemen that they were. It was impossible to have imagined the three playing on a line together thirty years earlier, with Howe still out there in his All-Star Game togs.

In the game, Howe drew an assist on Real Cloutier's goal in the third period. Howe made a nice pass from the corner to Cloutier in the slot, and he buried the puck to make it a 6–3 game for the Prince of Wales Conference over the Campbell Conference. Howe also had three shots on goal, nearly scoring in the first period. His slapshot was a rocket that was stopped awkwardly by the glove of Tony Esposito. Tony O had to leave the game, having aggravated a sore right hand while making the save.

WHY IT WON'T BE EQUALLED You can count on two hands the number of players who have even played in the NHL for twenty-three years. The number who have maintained a world-class level of play over that time, you can count on one finger—Gordie Howe. And, if the NHL's Olympic participation continues, that means one out of every four All-Star Games will be cancelled, so that to play in twenty-three games a player has to be active for some twenty-nine years. Not happening.

ALL-STAR FACTS The next most active All-Star player in the NHL is Ray Bourque, who played in nineteen All-Star Games. But Howe was also named to the year-end All-Star Team more than any other player. He was a First Team All-Star twelve times and Second Team selection nine times, the twenty-one total also unmatched. Bourque is second in that category as well, again with nineteen, though he does hold the record with thirteen First Team selections. No one else is close. Wayne Gretzky had fifteen selections (8 Firsts, 7 Seconds), and Maurice Richard had a total of fourteen (8 Firsts, 6 Seconds).

As well, Howe played in five decades, from the 1940s through the 1980s. Most incredible is to look at some of his teammates from his first All-Star Game in 1948. These included Milt Schmidt, Woody Dumart, Elmer Lach, and Maurice Richard. The All-Stars beat the Cup champion Leafs, 3–1. The Leafs' lineup had Turk Broda in goal, as well as Ted Kennedy and Harry Watson. It's amazing to be able to connect a star from the 1930s, like Schmidt was, to a star of the 1990s, like Gretzky, through Howe, who played with them both!

HOWE AND GRETZKY ENJOY A FRIENDLY CHAT DURING ALL-STAR GAME FESTIVITIES.

GRETZKY GETS 1,000TH POINT IN 424TH GAME

THE RECORD On December 19, 1984, midway through his sixth NHL season, Wayne Gretzky recorded his 1,000th career point during a six-point night in a 7–3 home win over Los Angeles. He reached the milestone in just 424 games.

HOW IT WAS DONE Gretzky redefined scoring during his career. Previously, if a player averaged two points a game for eight or ten games, he was "hot," playing great hockey, someone to watch out for. Gretzky averaged two points for twenty years. When he was "hot," he was averaging three or four points a game. In order for him to get to 1,000 career points, a Hall of Fame milestone for every player before or since, he had to be both prolific and consistent. In his first six seasons, he played 473 games of a possible 480, missing only seven because of injury. As well, he recorded points in all but forty-nine games. As a rookie, he was pointless in seventeen games, then twelve the next year, then eight, four, three, and five. In those 473 games, he had multi-point games 269 times. Finally, on December 19, 1984, he entered the game with 999 career points.

Everyone knew this night he would reach 1,000—a home game, just before Christmas, the

GETTING TO 2,000—HOW MANY GAMES?

How long did it take Gretzky to get his second thousand points? Well, he started on December 19, 1984, we know that. He got 2,000 on October 26, 1990, just 434 games later. To maintain this pace for 1,000 points was unheard of, but to get a second thousand points in virtually the exact same number of games is unfathomable. In between, Gretzky passed Gordie Howe as the all-time leading scorer in NHL history. That historic night came on October 15, 1989, when, now playing for Los Angeles, he returned to Edmonton for a game. He was twenty-seven years old. Howe was fifty-two when he got his 1,850th point. Gretzky was far from done, though.

Oilers on another roll. Gretzky wasted no time, setting up Mike Krushelnyski for a goal 1:41 into the game. That was 1,000, but his night wasn't done by any means. Gretzky added another goal and assist even before the first period was over, then added another assist in the second, and scored again with another assist in the third period. Six points, 1,005 career points. Already well on his way to a second thousand. In the crowd at Northlands Coliseum were his parents and brother, Brent.

WHY IT WON'T BE EQUALLED This record will live in the annals of the game for decades and longer simply because there is only one Wayne

Of course, Gretzky was not only fastest to 1,000 points, he also got goal number 500 faster than anyone. Of the forty-one players in NHL history to reach 500, only four have accomplished the feat in fewer than 700 games. Gretzky leads the way, having got number 500 on November 22, 1986, in just his 575th game. Not far behind, of course, was Mario, who needed only 605 games. Mike Bossy needed 647, and Brett Hull needed 693.

The most recent player to do it under 1,000 games was Finland's Teemu Selanne, who notched number 500 on November 22, 2006, in his 982nd game. What Bossy and Gretzky have in common, though, is that they are two of only four players who got number 500 by scoring into an empty net. The others were Jari Kurri and Keith Tkachuk. Gretzky finished with 894 goals. Next closest was, and still is, Gordie Howe, who had 801. Third is Brett Hull, with 741.

Gretzky. As well, goalies are better, coaching is better, scoring is well below the standards of the 1980s. Getting to 1,000 so quickly requires not only great skill; it requires being on a great team, staying healthy, and being consistent at an unbelievable level for many years. It requires the power of the sprinter but the durability of a marathoner.

GRETZKY RECORDS HIS 1,000TH CAREER POINT IN GAME NUMBER 424.

COMPARING THE OTHER GREATEST PLAYERS As with many of Gretzky's scoring records, the next closest player to reach 1,000 points was Mario Lemieux. He reached 1,000 in 513 games almost a decade after Gretzky, averaging slightly less than two points a game in the first six years of his career. In all, only twelve players got to 1,000 points before their 800th game, and all of them are Hall of Famers.

After that, the competition thins out quickly. Mike Bossy scored his 1,000th point in his 656th game, and Gretzky's longtime linemate, Jari Kurri, needed just 716 games, Guy Lafleur in his 720th, Bryan Trottier in his 726th game, and Denis Savard in his 727th are next on the list. Steve Yzerman checks in next in 737 games and Marcel Dionne needed 740 games. Phil Esposito, the only name on the list before Gretzky, time-wise, needed only 745 games when he got number 1,000 in 1974.

Jaromir Jagr, the second European on the list, needed 763 games, and Paul Coffey, the only defenceman on the list, was right behind at 770 games. Dale Hawerchuk at 781 is the final sub-800-game player on the list. All of these achievements, though incredible, pale beside Gretzky's 424 games.

"IRON MAN" DOUG JARVIS PLAYS 964 CONSECUTIVE GAMES

THE RECORD For more than twelve seasons, from October 8, 1975 to October 10, 1987, Doug Jarvis played every game, an Iron Man streak of 964 games.

HOW IT WAS DONE It isn't very often that a top player gets traded after being drafted but before playing even a few games with the team that drafted him, but that's exactly what happened to Doug Jarvis. After Toronto drafted him twenty-fourth overall in the 1975 Amateur Draft, they sent him to Montreal for Greg Hubick. Jarvis was a rookie in the Habs lineup at the start of 1975–76, playing his first game on October 8, 1975, and he was in the lineup every game for the next twelve years and more, with three teams.

The Habs traded him in a blockbuster deal during the summer of 1982, sending Jarvis, Rod Langway, and Brian Engblom to Washington for Ryan Walter and Rick Green. The Habs had won the Stanley Cup in each of Jarvis's first four years, but they were on a downswing soon after. Three and a half seasons later, the Caps sent him to Hartford for Jorgen Pettersson. It was there that he surpassed Garry Unger, who had played 914 games in a row, but after two games of the 1987–88 season Jarvis's streak was over.

The end of it came as no surprise to him. At the start of the season, the thirty-two-year-old sat down

STEVE LARMER SO CLOSE

The player who had the best chance to beat Jarvis, Steve Larmer had his Iron Man streak come to a grinding halt at the start of the 1993–94 season because of a contract dispute. Drafted by Chicago in 1980, he started his streak with the Hawks when he made the team full time at training camp in 1982. For the next eleven years and 884 regular-season games, he was in the lineup every night. He was also one of the league's top scorers, averaging thirty-seven goals a season in that time. His streak is a record for a player with one team, but he sat out the start of the 1993–94 season because he couldn't agree to terms with management on a new deal. The Hawks traded him to the Rangers, and they won the Stanley Cup that year. He lost his Iron Man record but won the only Cup of his career, a fair trade at the end of the day.

with coach Jack Evans to discuss his role on the team. He agreed that he was now a step slower and couldn't be expected to dress for all eighty games. On the morning of October 11, 1987, Evans told Jarvis he would be a healthy scratch and Brent Peterson would play instead that night against Boston. It was a bitter-sweet moment. "I don't think it'll sink in until I'm looking back someday after I'm finished as a player," he admitted after the game. "I wasn't going to play every game. That's reality right there."

OTHER IRON MEN

Of course, Cal Ripkin is the owner of the longest Iron Man streak, but given that baseball plays 162 games a year and is far less physically demanding, his 2,632 games streak with the Baltimore Orioles, while impressive, doesn't rival Jarvis's. A more impressive streak might be Brett Favre's. The quarterback played in 297 straight games (plus 24 post-season for a total of 321), an incredible record of durability considering the demands of the NFL and the extreme physicality of being a quarterback. A lesser-known basketballer named A.C. Green played in 1,192 straight NBA games. Unique is the career of Andy Hebenton. He played nine years in the NHL, from 1955 to 1964, and never missed a game, 630 in all. No other player with a career as long can boast as much.

The other reality was that he had been exposed in the NHL's Waiver Draft the previous week, but there were no takers among the other teams. He retired soon after, but what is most amazing about his streak is that he actually grew old before it came to an end. Time, not injury, was the Iron Man's nemesis.

WHY IT WON'T BE EQUALLED There are several reasons which put this out of reach of any ambitious player. First, the league has gotten much younger, and with a worldwide talent pool from which to draw now (not the case in Jarvis's days), a player's chance for just being in the NHL for twelve years are far slimmer. As well, the game is so much more physical and tougher that any player who dresses for even one full season now is a warrior. Another key to reaching this record is staying with one team where a player can develop a reputation and role that perhaps goes beyond his abilities. Fewer and fewer players stay a dozen years with a team any more. The current Iron Men in the NHL are Jay Bouwmeester of Calgary (438 in a row), and Henrik Sedin of Vancouver (432), the former having played for just two teams and the latter with one.

UNGER'S STREAK ENDS But for a different coach or scenario, Garry Unger might have gone past 914 games in a row. His streak began on February 24, 1968, while he was a member of the Toronto Maple Leafs, and continued without break until December 21, 1979, a span of more than a decade with four teams (after the Leafs came Detroit, St. Louis, and Atlanta). In fact, he was healthy, dressed, and on the players' bench for game number 915, on December 23, 1979, against St. Louis, but his coach in Atlanta, Al MacNeil, believed the streak had gotten bigger than the player or team, so he benched Unger the entire night. It was a strange situation.

The Flames were leading 7–3 late in the game and players were urging MacNeil to play Unger for even a single shift. Unger had hurt his shoulder on December 9, and played only a few shifts each game since. "I dressed Unger and waited to see what went on in the game," MacNeil explained. "If I thought he could have helped us, I would have used him." In the final minute, even the St. Louis crowd started to scream for Unger, but MacNeil didn't budge. "I don't want to hurt Garry Unger, but he won't play until his shoulder heals or his play comes back up to par. I didn't play him because I didn't feel his contribution to the team was what I thought Garry Unger should be giving."

It was the only game he missed all season. If he hadn't been benched, the streak would have been at 963 games. The next year, he was with the L.A. Kings for a season, and his career wound down with the Edmonton Oilers.

LARRY ROBINSON CHASES THE CUP TWENTY CONSECUTIVE PLAYOFF YEARS

THE RECORD Defenceman Larry Robinson played in the NHL for twenty years, and his team qualified for the playoffs every season, a record for consecutive post-season success.

HOW IT WAS DONE Drafted twentieth overall by Montreal in 1971, Larry Robinson played a year and a half in the minors with the team's AHL affiliate in Nova Scotia before being recalled midway through the 1972–73 season. When he started in the NHL, he proved beyond a doubt he was ready for the highest level. The Habs were in transition, going from the Jean Beliveau-led teams of the 1960's to a new era that included newcomers Guy Lafleur, Guy Lapointe, and Serge Savard. The team was coached by Scotty Bowman, who assumed duties at the start of the 1971–72 season, and the goalie was Ken Dryden, who had taken the hockey world by storm as a rookie in the 1971 playoffs when he led the team to a Stanley Cup win despite having only six regular-season games' worth of experience.

Robinson was the key to the new defence. Big, strong, and mobile, he was a complete player, valuable in his own end and capable offensively as well.

MOST PLAYOFF GAMES

Making the playoffs has become increasingly difficult in the last twenty years. In the early 1980s, when there were twenty-one teams, sixteen qualified for the post-season. Today, with thirty teams, sixteen still qualify. Whereas once it was relatively easy, now it is about a fifty—fifty chance. And, with parity across the league, no team can think itself so dominant as to assume a playoff spot is a given. Robinson's perfect playoff success rate is one of three exceptional playoff games records.

The other surely is most playoff years in a career, a record held by Chris Chelios with twenty-four. How many players have even been in the NHL for twenty-four seasons? Even Gordie Howe made "only" twenty playoff years in his twenty-six-year career. The other record, also belonging to Chelios, is most playoff games. He appeared in 266 games, ahead of Detroit defenceman Nicklas Lidstrom (258) and goalie Patrick Roy (247). One more season from Lidstrom, though, should give him the record.

But he wasn't fluid or dominating like Bobby Orr. He was most effective when being a responsible defenceman, killing penalties and anchoring the power play. He had a heavy shot from the point which always seemed to hit the net and handcuff goalies, creating scoring chances and rebounds for the team's forwards to take advantage of. Robinson was also tough as nails, but as the years passed he had to prove himself less and less as he earned respect around the league from players who were, frankly, intimidated by ''Big

CONSECUTIVE YEARS IN PLAYOFFS BY TEAM

The Bruins have both the longest consecutive streaks for qualifying for the playoffs and one of the longest for consecutive misses. They made the 1968 playoffs and every one thereafter for the next twenty-nine years, not missing the post-season until 1997. Just before this streak, though, they missed the playoffs for eight straight years (1960–67). Chicago qualified for twenty-eight straight years (1970–97), and Detroit has had two streaks of twenty years. The first came from 1939 to 1958, and the second is ongoing. After missing the playoffs in 1990, they have made it every year since, twenty and counting.

Montreal has had two lengthy streaks, one of twenty-four years (1971–94, during Robinson's career) and another of twenty-one years (1949–69). St. Louis had a streak of twenty-five years in a row (1980–2004), by far the most impressive of all post-Original Six teams. The Leafs' longest streak, for all their glorious past, was just fifteen years (1931–45). On the other hand, Florida now has missed the playoffs each of the last ten years and had made the playoffs only three times in its seventeen years of existence.

New Jersey also had a long streak of missing the playoffs before Martin Brodeur came on board, failing to qualify nine years in a row from 1979 to 1987. Calgary missed the playoffs for seven years (1997–2003), but the Flames also made the playoffs sixteen straight years (1976–91). At the start of the franchise, the hapless Washington Capitals missed the playoffs its first eight years of existence (1975–82).

ROBINSON PLAYED THREE SEASONS WITH LOS ANGELES AT THE END OF HIS CAREER.

Bird." Just as a team might maintain puck possession in the offensive end while changing lines, the Habs had the knack of rebuilding even as they continued to win.

Robinson was part of a new, young team that went on a run which saw them qualify for the post-season for each of the next twenty-four years after missing the playoffs in 1970 under odd circumstances. Robinson was part of seventeen years of that incredible streak, during which time he and the Habs won the Cup six times. Perhaps the most satisfying of those wins came in 1986, when the team was re-building again and was considered a longshot to go far in the playoffs. But riding another rookie sensation in goal, Patrick Roy, the team beat all comers in 1986, and the thirty-five-year-old Robinson felt a personal rejuvenation of sorts.

ROBINSON'S STELLAR PLAY AT THE 1984 CANADA CUP REJUVENATED HIS CAREER.

CANADA CUP GLORY

Because Robinson was in the playoffs every year of his career, the only chance he ever got to play for his country was at the Canada Cup. The World Championship, after all, was played concurrently with the playoffs, and at that time NHLers didn't play at the Olympics. Robinson appeared in each of the first three Canada Cups, 1976, 1981, and 1984, the last perhaps a career saver. He wasn't particularly effective in the inaugural event in 1976, failing to record a single point. But Canada won the tournament anyway thanks to Darryl Sittler's famous overtime goal against Czechoslovakia. In 1981, Canada suffered a humiliating 8–1 loss to the Soviets in the championship game.

In 1984, though, Robinson was stunned by the invitation to training camp extended to him by coach Glen Sather. The thirty-three-year-old had been in the league twelve years, and the game was now dominated by the high-flying Oilers. Robinson saw little sense in his being invited. But, he attended camp, was one of the best blue-liners there, and made the team. He was, if not dominating, then certainly very impressive in helping Canada win again, and he credited that event with revitalizing his career at a time Montreal was rebuilding and wasn't sure it even wanted Robinson around any longer.

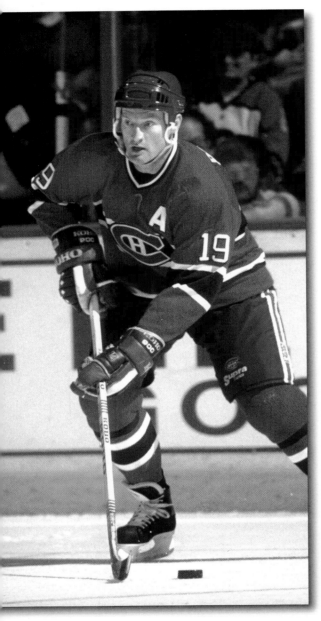

ROBINSON NEVER MISSED THE PLAYOFFS IN
SEVENTEEN SEASONS WITH MONTREAL.

By the end of the 1988–89 season, though, the Habs believed his best days were well behind him and they didn't re-sign him. While Robinson could have retired knowing his place in history had been set, he decided his love for the game outstripped his career statistics panel showing that he had played for only one team in his life. He signed with the Los Angeles Kings, a team that had made a splash by acquiring Wayne Gretzky. He played for three more years with the Kings, again making the playoffs every year and bringing his consecutive total to a record twenty. Robinson won the Norris Trophy twice and was named winner of the Conn Smythe Trophy in 1978.

WHY IT WON'T BE EQUALLED As with many of the greatest and most unbeatable records, this combines skill with a little luck and a ton of consistency over a long period of time. We can refer to the fact that only fifty-six players have ever stayed in the NHL for twenty years as a starting point. Then, to be on a great team(s) to qualify for the playoffs every year is a sensational accomplishment, and to be healthy enough to play each time is further testament to the record's degree of difficulty. Not Gretzky or Howe or Orr or Messier were on teams so consistently good that they made the playoffs every year. Most years? Yes. Every year? No. Only Robinson can and will forever be able to make that boast in a twenty-year career.

GRETZKY'S POINT TOTAL OUT OF THIS WORLD

THE RECORD By the time he retired in 1999, after twenty seasons in the NHL, Wayne Gretzky had set some sixty-one league records, only a few of which have been or will be bettered, and many of which will stand the test of time. First and foremost among these records is his career points total in the regular season—a staggering, eye-popping 2,857.

HOW IT WAS DONE Ever since he was a kid, Wayne Gretzky was destined to be the next great star of the NHL. But while many phenoms have been so labeled over the years, few have delivered the goods, as it were. And none has delivered to the degree "the Great One" did during his pro career. In his first NHL season, 1979–80, he scored fifty-one goals and 137 points, tied for tops in the league with Marcel Dionne. This was to be Gretzky's *lowest* point total for the next twelve years as he broke, and broke again, every major scoring record.

The next season he broke Bobby Orr's assist record and Phil Esposito's points record by collecting 164 points on the season (Orr had had 102 assists; Esposito 152 points). The year after that, Gretzky had 120 assists and 212 points. He was twenty-one years old. He eventually improved his records for goals scored to ninety-two, assists to 163, and points to 215, staggering achievements never to be equaled.

UNBEATABLE CAREER RECORDS

GRETZKY ALSO ALL-TIME "ALL LEAGUES" GOAL SCORING LEADER

Gretzky scored only nine goals in his final NHL season, but that ninth gave him another scoring record. It bettered by just one goal the all-time goal scoring totals of Gordie Howe for both NHL and WHA, and both regular season and playoffs. Howe had accumulated 1,071 goals in his thirty-two seasons of pro hockey, and when he retired, the Great One had exactly 1,072.

In all, he scored 200 points on four occasions, and on eleven occasions had more than 100 assists. Before his thirtieth birthday he was the all-time leader in all major offensive categories, surpassing Gordie Howe as the all-time leader in goals, assists, and points. Gretzky won the Art Ross Trophy an unprecedented ten times. By the time he retired in April 1999, Gretzky had 894 goals (to Howe's 801) and 1,963 assists.

Mark Messier eventually moved up to second on the scoring list with 1,887 points, but amazingly, Gretzky had more assists than either Howe or Messier had total points. In other words, even if Gretzky never scored a single goal during his twenty-year career, he still would have retired as the greatest point scorer in league history. And Gretzky earned his points in

HOW DOES IT COMPARE? One would think that because the NHL is the world's best hockey league, that other leagues of lesser calibre would have greater records because they would be more easily achieved. Not so. The American Hockey League, for instance, counts Willie Marshall as its all-time leader in points. He played in the AHL for twenty years (same length career as Gretzky), but he retired with 1,375 points in 1,205 games (including 523 goals), far less than half of Gretzky's totals. In Europe, the records pale all the more. Jorgen Jonsson, for instance, is the all-time scorer in Sweden's Elitserien, but he has a mere 658 points in 874 games spread over a seventeen-year career (1992–2009).

just 1,487 games, an average of nearly two points a game, every game, for twenty years. By comparison, Howe played 1,767 games and Messier 1,756.

WHY GRETZKY'S RECORD WON'T BE EQUALLED

The benchmark for a truly great player is 100 points in a season. For someone to break Gretzky's record, that player would have to record twenty-nine consecutive 100-point seasons. *Twenty-nine!* Okay, one might argue that great players sometimes score more than 100 points in a year. Still, a player would have to record 200 points a year for *fourteen seasons* just to come close to Gretzky's record. The trouble with that achievement is that 200 points in a season has been accomplished only four times—all by Gretzky himself. In fact, nine of the top eleven point scoring seasons in NHL history have been recorded by Gretzky, the only player to keep similar company being Mario Lemieux.

Gordie Howe took twenty-six seasons to earn his 1,850 points; Gretzky took five seasons less to better Howe's record by more than 50 per cent. Howe was the first NHLer to score 1,000 career points, a milestone he hit in his 938th game. Gretzky hit 1,000 in game number 424, less than half the time. Coincidentally, Howe's last NHL season was Gretzky's first. If a player wants to erase the name "Gretzky" from one of his sixty-one NHL records, he had better look to achievements other than 2,857 career points. This is in the books forever.

WAYNE VS. VIKING, ALBERTA

How does Gretzky's totals stack up against the six Sutters who played in the NHL? Well, the family is the superior scoring unit—but not by much. In all, Brent, Brian, Darryl, Duane, Rich, and Ron Sutter all made it to the NHL, the largest hockey family in NHL history. They combined to play an incredible eighty-one NHL seasons and 4,994 regular-season games, during which time they accumulated 2,934 points, just seventy-seven more than Gretzky.

NUMBER 802! GRETZKY'S GOAL AGAINST VANCOUVER ON MARCH 23, 1994 MADE HIM THE NHL'S ALL-TIME LEADING GOALSCORER.

RECORDS FOREVER

"THE GREAT ONE" RETIRES WITH 382 CAREER PLAYOFF POINTS

THE RECORD By the time he hung up his skates in 1999, Wayne Gretzky had appeared in 208 playoff games and registered 382 playoff points, nearly 100 more than the second-ranked player (teammate Mark Messier, with 295). These totals include 122 goals and 260 assists.

HOW IT WAS DONE The only way to accumulate 382 playoff points in a career is to play a long time, make the playoffs a lot, go deep into the playoffs a lot—and score like crazy. Gretzky played twenty NHL seasons and made the playoffs sixteen times, averaging twelve playoff games a season.

Gretzky made it to the Stanley Cup Final six times. He has four of the top five playoff-points totals in league history; a record forty-seven points in 1985, with Edmonton; forty-three points in 1988; forty points in 1993, with Los Angeles; and, thirty-eight points in 1983. The only other player nestled in among this historic quintet of great playoff seasons is Mario Lemieux, who had forty-four points with Pittsburgh in 1991.

Gretzky and the Oilers had to learn the hard way how to win in the playoffs. In his first season, 1979–80, the Flyers eliminated Edmonton in three straight games in the best-of-five preliminary round. Gretzky

MARK MESSIER HOLDS THE STANLEY CUP IN 1990.

had all of two goals and one assist in the series. The next year, the Oilers swept the Habs in three but lost to the Islanders in six games in the next round. In 1981–82, they took the L.A. Kings too lightly and lost in the first round. But 1983 was a turning point for the team. The Oilers went all the way to the Stanley Cup Final, only to be hammered by the Islanders' dynasty in four straight.

Gretzky set a playoff record with thirty-eight points that year, but he was held without a goal in the Final, recording four assists on just six Edmonton goals in the series. That loss taught Gretzky what it took to win, and he led the team to four Stanley Cup wins in the next five years. He led the playoffs in scoring on six occasions (tied for the most with Gordie Howe), but only one of those came after being traded away from the Oilers in 1988. That was in 1993 when he took the L.A. Kings to the Final for the first and only time in franchise history.

WHY IT WON'T BE EQUALLED With thirty teams in the NHL, it has become more difficult to make it into the playoffs on a regular basis. And with parity, a salary cap, and expert coaching, top teams cannot routinely count on going to the semi-finals

COMBINED POINTS Gretzky's 2,857 regular-season points combined with 382 playoff points give him a total of 3,239 total NHL points. Second is longtime teammate, Mark Messier, with 2,182 combined points, and third is Howe, with 2,010. Under-appreciated Ron Francis is fourth with 1,941, and rounding out the top five is Steve Yzerman, with 1,940. In all, Gretzky scored 1,016 goals and 2,223 assists, his assists total alone more than Messier's points total.

ACTIVE LEADERS

No player currently in the NHL is remotely close to Gretzky's record. The active leader is Detroit defenceman Nicklas Lidstrom who, at forty-one years of age, has 183 playoff points. A future Hall of Famer and brilliant player, his total is less than half of Gretzky's. Second is Mark Recchi, with 148, but the forty-three-year-old retired in the summer of 2011 after winning the Cup with Boston. Third is forty-one-year-old Mike Modano, with 145. Next is thirty-eight-year-old defenceman Chris Pronger, with 120. New Jersey forward Patrik Elias has 117, but at thirty-five years of age he also won't come close to Gretzky.

THE BEST OF THE LAST FIFTEEN SEASONS

If you add the points totals for the leading scorers in the playoffs the last fifteen years, the total would be 377 points, still shy of Gretzky's record. Of course, all of those fifteen scoring leaders (with one exception) went to the Cup Final. Even Gretzky led the playoff scoring race "only" six times, and no player has ever made it to the Cup Final fifteen straight years. The possibility of someone playing as many games and scoring almost two points a game for fifteen playoff years is simply an untenable hypothesis. Even just playing 208 playoff games is itself incredible, something accomplished only thirteen times.

or Final every year. In the last fifteen years, only two players have even reached thirty points in a playoff year—Pittsburgh's Evgeni Malkin, with thirty-six in 2008–09, and Daniel Briere, with thirty for Philadelphia in 2009–10. So, despite thirty points being a difficult goal for any one playoff year, a player would have to record thirty points for thirteen playoff years in his career to surpass Gretzky's career total. In one sentence—that's not going to happen.

GRETZKY WON THE CUP FOUR TIMES WITH THE OILERS IN THE 1980S.

"SCOTTY" BOWMAN COACHES 2,494 GAMES

THE RECORD From the time he coached his first NHL game in 1967 until he coached his last game in 2002, Scotty Bowman was building a legacy of success and longevity that no coach will ever equal. In all, he was behind the bench for 2,141 regular-season games, 353 more in the playoffs, and nine Stanley Cup victories. All are records that can be classified as untouchable.

HOW IT WAS DONE There are only two ingredients to establish a record the likes of what Scotty Bowman did—coach a long time and win the vast majority of games. Bowman began coaching at age thirty-four in 1967 with St. Louis, taking over for Lynn Patrick early in the season. He stayed for parts of four years, taking the expansion team from its first baby steps in the league to becoming a mature team that went to the Stanley Cup Final in each of its first three seasons. At the time, the Original Six teams were in one division while the six expansion teams were in the other. This ensured an expansion team would be in the Cup Final. The Blues lost all twelve Cup Final games they played during this run, but it was they and no other of the new teams that advanced to the Final.

Despite taking over a new franchise, Bowman had a winning record in each of these four seasons. He left in the summer of 1971 to coach the Canadiens, hired by general manager Sam Pollock who had given

Bowman his first coaching job with the Habs' farm team prior to expansion. Bowman stayed with the Habs for seven seasons, winning the Cup five times and compiling an impressive record along the way. In all, he coached 634 regular-season games with the Canadiens, winning a staggering 419 and losing only 110. This included the historic 1976–77 season in which the Habs had a 60–8–12 record, the best ever.

When he didn't get the GM job after Pollock retired, Bowman left the Habs for Buffalo. At first, he didn't want to coach the Sabres; he wanted only to be the team's GM. But it soon became apparent he could do the coaching job better than anyone, and he found himself back behind the bench. He was there for four full seasons and parts of three others, having a losing record only in his final year, 1986–87, when the team was 3–7–2 in its first twelve games.

Bowman then ended up coaching in Pittsburgh for two years. Again, after he thought he had left the bench and moved to the front office for good, he had to take over coaching duties after the sudden death of Bob Johnson. In 1993, the Detroit Red Wings hired him, and for the next nine years he helped transform the team into a perennial contender, winning the Cup three more times before retiring for good in 2002.

Those few games in 1986–87 represented the only time he had a losing record in thirty years behind the bench. He set records for most games coached and won in the regular season, and most games coached and won in the playoffs as well.

WHY IT WON'T BE EQUALLED

Just to coach 2,141 games would require a coach to last more than twenty-six seasons in an eighty-two-game schedule. Given that the shelf life of a coach is only about two or three years with any one team, the sheer ability to last a quarter century is almost impossible in itself. Then, factor in thirty NHL teams fighting for sixteen playoff spots. A nearly 50 per cent rate of failure every year to qualify for the post-season means a commensurate number of coaching changes.

Of course, anyone able to stay in coaching for twenty-six years must also be able to win for twenty-six years, a quality no other coach has proved capable of for as long. And, for a coach to last 353 playoff games would mean going to the Cup Final for about fourteen consecutive years (averaging a Cup run to be about twenty-five games). That's just not going to happen. As well, coaches, like players, are getting younger, so the chances of a coach lasting thirty years is slim to none, for even if the coach wanted to stick around that long, young GMs wouldn't be so quick to agree.

Bowman has his name on the Stanley Cup for three other victories. The 1991 Pittsburgh win was added to his resume because he was director of player development for the team that year. In 2008, he was a consultant for the Detroit Red Wings, and in 2010 he was senior advisor of hockey operations for Chicago. Bowman left Detroit for Chicago in the summer of 2008 because his son, Stan, was the Hawks' general manager. They became the first father-son team to win the Stanley Cup. Scotty's son is named Stanley Glenn Bowman. He was born in June 1973, shortly after the Habs won the Cup with Scotty as coach. He named his son Stanley, because of the trophy, and Glenn because of his great admiration for goalie Glenn Hall, whom Scotty had coached during his first years behind the bench with the expansion St. Louis Blues.

AL ARBOUR WAS ONE OF THE GREATEST COACHES IN LEAGUE HISTORY DURING HIS TENURE WITH THE NEW YORK ISLANDERS.

THE CONTENDERS Al Arbour lasted twenty-two years behind the bench for the New York Islanders, but his 1,606 games coached and 781 victories pale in comparison to Bowman's achievements. Dick Irvin coached Toronto, Montreal, and Chicago for twenty-seven years, but with a shorter schedule in the old days that amounted to 1,449 games. As for active coaches, Toronto's Ron Wilson has reached the 1,300-game mark and 600-win mark, and fifty-one-year-old Lindy Ruff has passed 1,000. Paul Maurice stands at 1,059 after the 2010–11 season, and he has as good a chance as any to catch Bowman only because he's only forty-four years old. However, he's had a winning record in only seven of his fourteen seasons, so if he's going to last another fourteen, he's likely going to have to win more often.

The fifty-three-year-old Joel Quenneville is another top contender. He won the Cup with Chicago in 2010 and has a great young team which could keep going for many more years. He's coached 1,081 games as of the end of 2010–11, but he is still far short of 600 victories for his own career. Marc Crawford, recently fired from Dallas, has 1,151 games coached to his credit and might get near Bowman if he stays around long enough. There are many great coaches who have been around a long time, but none will win 1,200 games in their lifetimes.

RECORDS FOREVER

MIKE SILLINGER PLAYS FOR TWELVE TEAMS

THE RECORD In an NHL career that started in 1990 and continued until 2009, Mike Sillinger dressed for twelve NHL teams, more than any other player in league history.

HOW IT WAS DONE Some records aren't really broken so much as created out of the natural order of things: they just happen. Such can be said for Sillinger, who started his career with a fair degree of normalcy. Drafted by Detroit in 1989, he made his debut with the Red Wings on October 4, 1990. He stayed three games before being returned to junior, in Regina. The next year, he appeared only in the play-offs for the Red Wings, and then, briefly. He played parts of two and a half more years with the team and then was traded to Anaheim on April 4, 1995, towards the end of the lockout-shortened season.

That's when things started to go a little awry. After parts of two seasons with the Ducks, Sillinger was traded again, this time to Vancouver. After 138 games, another trade sent him to Philadelphia, and just fifty-two games later, Tampa Bay. Parts of two seasons took him across state to the Florida Panthers, and at the next trade deadline he was off to Ottawa. He played only thirteen games with the Senators before

EXPLAINING SILLINGER'S PERIPATETIC CAREER

On April 4, 1995, the Mighty Ducks of Anaheim made a big push, trading Stu Grimson, Mark Ferner, and a sixth-round draft choice in 1996 to Detroit for Mike Sillinger and Jason York. Sillinger was happy with the trade. In fact, he had been a healthy scratch the last fifteen Red Wings games and requested a trade because the team was so deep at centre, already having Steve Yzerman, Sergei Fedorov, Kris Draper, and Keith Primeau.

Sillinger was acquired by Vancouver on March 15, 1996, from Anaheim for Roman Oksiuta. "I'm a western boy, and I always thought I'd like to go back and play in Canada," he said. "I'm starting to come to the age when I should be getting into my prime. Usually, when there's rumours, you don't get traded. I didn't hear any rumours, so I got traded. That's how it goes. I was very surprised, but I'm happy to be a Vancouver Canuck."

On being traded from Vancouver to Philadelphia, on February 5, 1998: "Basically, he [Canucks coach Mike Keenan] didn't like my size. He likes players over six feet. I'm a right wing and centre, and that's what I'm going to bring to this team. I'm a versatile guy. I can play the penalty kill, the power play, even left wing. I guess you could say I've done it all. Mike did me a favour trading me to this team."

On December 12, 1998, Sillinger and Chris Gratton were traded to Tampa Bay. Gratton made his debut with the Lightning that night, but Sillinger was Christmas shopping in Toronto when the deal was made and couldn't get a flight out in time.

The Panthers acquired Mike Sillinger from Tampa Bay for Ryan Johnson and Dwayne Hay near the trade deadline. "This, to me, is new life," he said once the deal was announced. "It's something to play for. With the playoffs coming and knowing that I'm going to a great team that can really do some damage when we get to the post-season, I just can't tell you how geared up I am."

continued on page 67

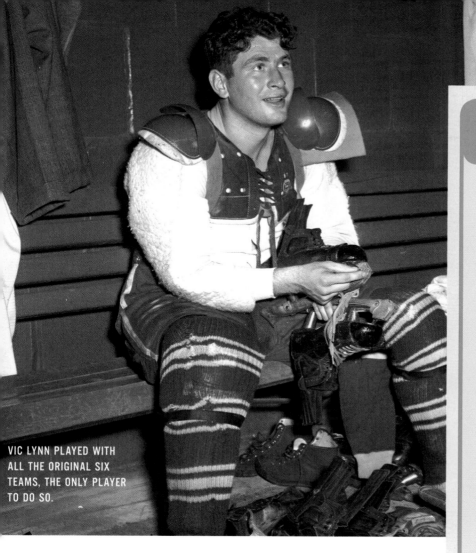

VIC LYNN PLAYED WITH ALL THE ORIGINAL SIX TEAMS, THE ONLY PLAYER TO DO SO.

THE ENTIRE ORIGINAL SIX

The truly unique player from the Original Six was Vic Lynn. The Saskatoon native was the only player to appear for all six teams during the glory days of the NHL. He started with the Rangers in 1942–43, playing a single game, and then joined the Red Wings the following year for three games. Two years later, he had another brief appearance, this time playing just twice with Montreal. He then established himself with the Leafs, staying for four years and helping them win the Stanley Cup three years running, 1947–49. The Leafs then traded him to Boston, where he dressed for sixty-eight games over two seasons, and Chicago acquired him in early 1953. He played parts of two seasons for the Hawks before returning to Saskatoon and enjoying a lengthy career in senior hockey.

signing with Columbus as a free agent in the summer of 2001. He was then traded twice in the summer of 2003 on the same day, going first to Dallas and then to Phoenix. He didn't last the season with the Coyotes before being shipped to St. Louis. After the lockout, the Blues traded him to Nashville, and in the summer of 2006, he signed as a free agent with the New York Islanders. Injuries forced him to retire in 2009 after twelve teams and 1,049 games.

WHY IT WON'T BE EQUALLED

Perhaps towards the end of his career, Sillinger should have won the Masterton Trophy for perseverance. How else can one explain the patience and dedication needed to handle one move after another? No player has been traded as often, and although it's easy to say it's possible for someone else to come along and play for thirteen teams, the likelihood is so remote and the determination to play for so many teams so rare, that Sillinger is likely in the record books forever.

RUNNERS-UP

Michel Petit and J-J Daigneault have played for the second-most NHL teams, ten each. In the case of Petit, he started with Vancouver in 1982 after the Canucks had drafted him eleventh overall earlier that year. He went on to play for the New York Rangers, Quebec Nordiques, Toronto, Calgary, Los Angeles, Tampa Bay, Edmonton, Philadelphia, and Phoenix. In Daigneault's case, he also started off with the Canucks, in 1984. They, too, had drafted him that same June. He went on to play for Philadelphia, Montreal, St. Louis, Pittsburgh, Anaheim, New York Islanders, Nashville, Phoenix, and Minnesota. Neither player, however, made it to 1,000 career games.

PLAYOFFS Sillinger also holds the record of playing for the most teams in the post-season, with eight, though he never came particularly close to winning the Stanley Cup. He dressed for the Red Wings in the 1991 and 1992 playoffs, appearing in three and eight games, respectively, but never making it past the second round. He didn't make it back to the post-season again until 1996, with Vancouver, but the Canucks lost in the first round to Colorado who were en route to their first Stanley Cup. Sillinger played all six games of the series, at any rate.

Two years later, with the Flyers, he played three of five games, but the Flyers lost to Buffalo. Fast forward to the year 2000, with Florida, and he was in every game of a four-game sweep by New Jersey. The next year, with Ottawa, the pattern repeated. The Senators were swept by the Leafs, and Sillinger was on ice for every loss. St. Louis lost to San Jose in five games in 2004; in 2006, San Jose beat Nashville in five games; and, in 2007, the Islanders lost to Buffalo in five games. When all is added up, Sillinger played in forty-three playoff games.

continued from page 64

The Senators beefed up their roster in the hopes of a long playoff run, adding Mike Sillinger and Curtis Leschyshyn from Florida on March 13, 2001. "It's everyone's dream to win the Stanley Cup," Sillinger enthused. "I'm not worried about signing a contract. My goal [in Florida] was to sign a contract because there was no other goal. Now, my goal is to win the Stanley Cup."

Sillinger signed a three-year, $5.25 million contract with Columbus on July 5, 2001, hoping he and Ray Whitney, a teammate in his Florida days, could work a little magic together. "Passing the puck and reading the plays, Ray and I just both think very similarly," Sillinger explained. "I know if we play together, it'll be a hard-working line. Hopefully it's a line that'll put up a lot of points, too."

A double deal occurred on July 22, 2003. Dallas traded Darryl Sydor to Columbus for Mike Sillinger and a second-round draft choice in 2004, and then Phoenix sent Teppo Numminen to Dallas for Sillinger and a conditional draft choice in 2004. "I'm a hard worker, and I'm very competitive. I've been known as that throughout my career, wherever I've played...I'm excited. I talked to [GM] Mike Barnett, and he said they want players who are very competitive. They have good, young talent, and they think I can help not only out on the ice, but in the locker room."

Phoenix traded Sillinger to St. Louis on March 4, 2004, for goalie Brent Johnson. "I'm very used to it," Sillinger said upon learning of the deal. "I was kind of expecting it. It's the way my career has gone. Every couple of years I end up moving."

Sillinger was traded to Nashville on January 30, 2006, from St. Louis. "Hopefully everyone will understand I'm there to make the team better. I'm not there to take anyone's ice time. I'm there to help the team win, not only with my performance on the ice but as far as leadership in the locker room as well. Nashville has a very young team, and you're going to need some veteran leadership going into the playoffs."

On July 2, 2006, Sillinger signed as a free agent with the New York Islanders. Said GM Neil Smith: "Mike Sillinger is one of the most respected players in the game, strong in all zones and at faceoffs, an excellent skater and a leader." It was the last NHL team of Sillinger's career.

MARTIN BRODEUR PASSES TERRY SAWCHUK FOR CAREER SHUTOUTS

THE RECORD Martin Brodeur is still active, so every time he records a shutout he betters his own record by one. But on December 21, 2009, he recorded his 104th career shutout in the regular season to surpass Terry Sawchuk, a record that stood for thirty-nine years and one that most fans thought would never be broken.

HOW IT WAS DONE There is no simple or easy way to attain this record. No one-night miracle or hot streak is going to get a goalie to arguably the most difficult record in hockey. Brodeur got his first shutout on October 20, 1993, at age twenty-one, in a 4–0 win over Anaheim. He had played for New Jersey's farm team in Utica the previous year but at training camp in 1993, he proved himself a worthy backup to Chris Terreri. Brodeur had three shutouts that season and played his way into the number-one goalie position, winning more games and having a better GAA than the twenty-nine-year-old Terreri. Brodeur had three shutouts the next year as the clear number-one man, starting forty of forty-eight games in the lockout-shortened season.

In 1995–96, clearly one of the best young goalies in the league, Brodeur started seventy games and recorded six shutouts. Any inkling that he would become shutout king started the year after when he posted ten of them and repeated the feat in the next two seasons. He had eleven in 2003–04 and twelve in 2006–07, and on December 7, 2009, sixteen years after his first, he recorded his record-tying 103rd, in a 3–0 win over Buffalo. Two weeks later, he made history when he blanked Sidney Crosby and the Pittsburgh Penguins, 4–0, in Pennsylvania. Although Pittsburgh outshot the Devils, 35–30, Brodeur had an easier night than Marc-Andre Fleury.

In a classy gesture at the end of the game which produced the 104th shutout, a congratulatory message from Penguins owner Mario Lemieux was read over the p.a. system in Pittsburgh, which brought enthusiastic applause from the crowd at Mellon Arena. Said Crosby: "He's a legendary goalie, and he proves it every year. He's been so consistent, and that says a lot when you're able to get that many [shutouts]." Crosby tried his best to prevent the record, hitting the post with less than two minutes to play. But Brodeur still had plenty of hockey left in him, and as the end of the 2010–11 season came and went he had increased his regular-season total to 116 with no end in sight.

Brodeur is the only goalie other than Vladislav Tretiak to have won more than one Olympic gold medal, thanks to wins by Team Canada in Salt Lake City in 2002 and Vancouver in 2010. He also led Canada to victory at the World Cup of Hockey in 2004 and has taken New Jersey to the Stanley Cup three times. He has played in goal for one team longer than any other goalie, and he is tied with Ron Hextall for most goals by a goalie, each having shot the puck into the opposing net once in the regular season and once in the playoffs.

WHY IT WON'T BE EQUALLED

Like most of the toughest career records, this requires both consistency and the highest level of play, a difficult combination. It also requires incredible durability. Brodeur has been fortunate enough to be the number-one goalie almost from the day he played his first game. Twelve times he has played at least seventy games a season, something no coach would

MARTIN BRODEUR CELEBRATES OLYMPIC GOLD VICTORY WITH TEAMMATES AT SALT LAKE CITY IN 2002.

have permitted had he not demonstrated an ability to perform exceptionally while showing no fatigue. Few goalies in the game's history have exuded—and been given—such confidence over such a long career.

Even if a goalie recorded ten shutouts a season—an extraordinary achievement—he would need twelve straight seasons to usurp Brodeur. If Sawchuk's record lasted thirty-nine years and was considered unbeatable at 103, what does 116 and more constitute? Virtually impossible, that's what. And, we don't know when the record will end. Broduer has given no indication of retiring or slowing down. In 2010–11, at age thirty-eight, he was among the league leaders with six shutouts.

THE BRODEUR RECORD BOOK In addition to most regular-season shutouts, Brodeur holds every goalie record of importance except most playoff games played. Patrick Roy still towers over that record, having played 247 games. Brodeur is next at 181, and he likely won't catch Roy. However, Brodeur holds the records in the regular season for most games played (1,132 and counting), most minutes played (66,636 and counting), and most wins (625 and counting).

When he got win number 552 to surpass Patrick Roy, on March 17, 2009, at home against Chicago, teammates mobbed him at the final horn and gave him a pair of scissors. They, and the large crowd in New Jersey, then watched as he cut out the goal net from his end of the ice, the best memento a goalie could have after such an historic victory. Brodeur also holds the record for the most forty-win seasons (eight—next closest is three shared by four goalies), most thirty-win seasons (twelve—next closest is eight, Patrick Roy), and most wins in a season (forty-eight, set in 2006–07). He is tied with Roy for most playoff shutouts (23), and of course he has most total shutouts (regular season and playoffs—139 and counting).

All of these records are pretty much out of the reach of this generation of goalies, and for anyone to beat them a goalie will have to start young, play seventy or more games for fifteen seasons, have a tremendous defence for all those years—and be a Hall of Fame goalie as well.

MARTIN BRODEUR
STARTS 170 CONSECUTIVE PLAYOFF GAMES

THE RECORD Starting on May 15, 1994, Martin Brodeur has been the starting goalie in every playoff game for New Jersey, a streak spanning fifteen playoff seasons, three Stanley Cups, and 170 consecutive games.

HOW IT WAS DONE After being drafted twentieth overall by New Jersey in 1990, Brodeur stayed in the QMJHL with St. Hyacinthe for another two years. He was called up for four games in 1991–92 to get a taste of the NHL, and he appeared in his first playoff game that spring. In 1992–93, he played exclusively for the Devils' AHL affiliate, in Utica, and the next year he made the NHL team, sharing goaltending duties equally with Chris Terreri, the senior of the two by eight years.

In the 1994 playoffs, the Devils had a seven-game series with Buffalo. Brodeur played every minute of that series, and the Devils won the deciding game, 2–1, to set up a meeting with Boston in the next round. Coach Jacques Lemaire decided to split the goaltending chores for that six-game series, won by New Jersey, starting Brodeur in the first, second and fifth games, and Terreri in the other three. But beginning with the next series against the Rangers, a heart-breaking loss in seven games of the semi-finals, Brodeur started every remaining game, and every game since.

This run included four trips to the Stanley Cup Final, the aforementioned run to the semis, three years of play through two rounds of the post-season, and seven first-round losses, in all, an incredible thirty-two playoff series. The Devils missed the playoffs only twice, first in 1996 and then again this past season. During the seventeen years of his streak, Brodeur did occasionally get the hook in a game, but every time he was back in to start the following game.

SOME MARTY FACTS

During his 170-game streak (which is still counting), Brodeur has played more than 11,000 minutes and allowed, on average, fewer than two goals a game. He has twenty-two shutouts in that time, and in 2003 he set a record that might never be beat by registering seven shutouts in one playoff year. He also shares the record for most shutouts in one playoff series (3) with twelve others. Brodeur, however, is the only goalie to do it twice, in 1995 versus Boston and 2003 against Anaheim. The most surprising fact, though, is that he has played thirty-three overtime games during the streak and won only twelve, losing twenty-one, a surprisingly poor record given his incredible career.

WHY IT WON'T BE EQUALLED For a goalie even to be playing long enough to participate in fifteen playoffs is extraordinary. By and large, he is one of two goalies on a team, along with seven defencemen and thirteen forwards, so statistically it is a fact that his career is shorter than that of a skater. Then, to be so much the superior of the two goalies on his team that he gets the coach's confidence as the starter each and every game is even more unlikely. And, of course, the goalie must play well every game. A bad game would give the coach easy freedom to change goalies for the next game. As well, the team has to be good enough to play at least two rounds every one of those fifteen seasons simple to accumulate 170 total games played.

LONGEST SHUTOUT STREAK IN THE PLAYOFFS

No goalie can touch George Hainsworth's outstanding play in the 1930 playoffs with Montreal. He played shutout hockey for 270:08 against the Rangers and Boston. Dave Kerr of the Rangers had a streak of 248:35 in 1937, and in 1936 Normie Smith didn't allow a goal for Detroit in 248:32. J-S Giguere had a more contemporary streak in 2003, with Anaheim. The Ducks' goalie went 217:54 without allowing a goal, the longest streak since 1951 when Montreal's Gerry McNeil went 218:42. Brodeur later surpassed Giguere but didn't quite catch McNeil.

GEORGE HAINSWORTH.

RECORDS FOREVER

CRITICAL SHUTOUTS IN 2003

When Brodeur set a record with seven shutouts in the 2003 playoffs, he did so en route to his third Stanley Cup with the Devils. In each Cup year, he won all sixteen games for the team, of course, and his GAA those years was 1.67 (in 1995), 1.61 (in 2000), and 1.65 (in 2003). Brodeur got his first two shutouts in 2003 in the final two games of the opening series, shutting down the Bruins for the final 146:01 of the series in the five-game victory. He then shut out Tampa in the opening game of the next series, finally allowing a goal at 12:25 of the first period in game two and ending his shutout sequence at 218:26.

He got his fourth shutout of the playoffs in game two of the Conference finals against Ottawa, and got his fifth and sixth at the start of the Cup Final, against Anaheim. The Ducks didn't score their first goal of the series until midway through the second period of game three, ending another impressive streak of 161:46 of goalless hockey for Brodeur. Putting an accent on his season, he shut out the Ducks a third time in the final game of the year to win the Stanley Cup.

SIX SUTTERS—
AND THEN SONS

THE RECORD Six brothers from Viking, Alberta played in the NHL at the same time, and now the Sutter family has sent two second generation Sutters to the NHL—with more to follow.

THE SIX SUTTER BROTHERS (TOP, L-R) RON, RICH, BRENT; (BOTTOM, L-R) DUANE, BRIAN, DARRYL.

HOW IT WAS DONE The hockey world changed forever when Brian Sutter was called up from Kansas City of the CHL to play for the St. Louis Blues during the 1976–77 season. Selected twentieth overall by the Blues at the 1976 Amateur Draft, he would be the first of six brothers to play in the NHL. He was soon followed by Darryl (Chicago) and Duane (Islanders) in 1979–80, Brent (Islanders) in 1980–81, and then twins Rich (Pittsburgh) and Ron (Philadelphia), in 1982–83. The six brothers had an older brother, Gary, who they say was the best player of them all, but he gave up on a pro career early and stayed on the family farm in Viking.

From 1982 to 1987, all six Sutters were in the NHL at the same time, and then their careers started to end, and their numbers decreased. Darryl retired in 1987 and Brian a year later. Duane lasted until 1990 and Rich 1995. Brent hung up his skates in 1998, and Ron was the last to retire, playing until 2001. By this time, the family's cumulative games played reached almost 5,000.

They stayed in hockey and coached or scouted. Brian was the first to go behind the bench, with the Blues, in 1988. In all, he coached five teams for thirteen years and 1,028 regular-season games. Darryl coached in the NHL for a dozen years with Chicago, San Jose, and Calgary. Brent had an outstanding coaching career with Red Deer in the WHL until 2007 when he moved up to the NHL with New Jersey (and later Calgary). Duane had the shortest NHL coaching record, with Florida for only two years between 2000–02. Rich and Ron, ever the twins, never coached but both have gone into scouting.

As they aged, they started families of their own and now have six sons who have gone on to play hockey, two so far having made it to the NHL. Brandon, Brent's son, has played with Carolina since 2008 and Brett started with Calgary but has since traded to Carolina as well. Shaun, Brian's son, was drafted 102nd overall by Calgary in 1998 but never made it to the NHL. Merrick, Brent's son, played at U.S. college but never made it to the NHL either. Brody, Duane's son, is in the WHL and a legitimate prospect after being drafted

CLAN GEOFFRION

When Blake Geoffrion made his NHL debut on February 26, 2011, for the Nashville Predators, he made family, and NHL, history. Drafted fifty-sixth overall by the Predators in 2006, he was the son of Dan Geoffrion, who had a brief NHL career with Montreal and Winnipeg from 1979 to 1982, playing 111 regular-season games. Dan was the son of Bernie "Boom Boom" Geoffrion, a Hall of Famer who played with the Canadiens for most of his sixteen NHL seasons. "Boom Boom" was known for his slap shot and was only the second player to score fifty goals in a season. During the early days of his career, Bernie married Marlene Morenz, the daughter of the legendary Howie Morenz. As a result, Blake became the fourth generation of his family to make it to the NHL.

BLAKE GEOFFRION.

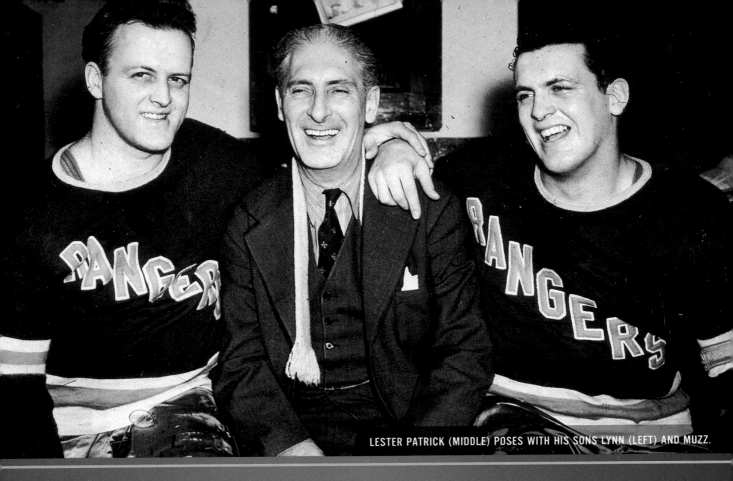

LESTER PATRICK (MIDDLE) POSES WITH HIS SONS LYNN (LEFT) AND MUZZ.

OTHER NOTABLE FAMILIES The Howe family has the distinction of being the only father and sons to play together in the NHL. This was achieved when Mark and Marty laced up with Gordie for the Hartford Whalers in the 1979–80 season. More recently, the Staal family of Thunder Bay has been impressive, Eric, Jordan, and Marc are all NHLers, while the youngest son Jared is hoping to be the fourth in the family to make it. Jared was drafted by Phoenix in 2008, but the twenty-one-year-old has yet to be called up to the big team.

The Patrick family is another three-generation representative in the NHL, starting with Lester Patrick who played briefly for the Rangers in the 1920s. His sons, Lynn and Muzz, went on to play in the NHL, as did Lynn's son, Craig. Without question the most interesting father-son combination is the Sullivan family, for reasons opposite to the Sutters. The patriarch Frank played for Canada at the 1928 Olympics (but never played in the NHL). He had two sons many years apart who did play in the NHL, though. Frank, Jr. started his career with the Leafs in 1949–50, and his brother, Peter, didn't make his NHL debut until thirty years later, with Winnipeg, in 1979–80! No brothers have made their NHL debuts so far apart.

193rd overall by Carolina in 2011, and Luke, Rich's son, has been playing in the USA Hockey system, the first of the family to plant American roots.

WHY IT WON'T BE EQUALLED

The average size of a family in both North America and Europe is falling, and parents find it too difficult to afford large families. Now consider the couples who do have large families—how many have six boys? And how many parents can even afford to put six boys through hockey? Combine these societal facts with the difficulty of developing even one boy into an NHL calibre player. How rare is it to have six become world-class players? It's a far rarer possibility than having quintuplets, winning the lottery, or flying to the moon. Is it possible for another Sutter family to come into this world? Sure—but the odds are astronomically against it.

While the Sutters had six brothers in the NHL at one time, the Hextall family is famous for its longevity. The first Hextall to play in the NHL was Bryan, who played with the Rangers from 1936 to 1948. He had two sons who went on to impressive NHL careers—Bryan, Jr. played with five teams from 1962 to 1976, and Dennis played with six teams from 1967 to 1980. Bryan, Jr. then had a son, Ron, who also left his mark on the NHL.

Ron Hextall was a goalie with Philadelphia, Quebec, and the New York Islanders from 1986 to 1999. He was known for extraordinary puck-handling ability as well as a mean streak that went well beyond the accepted boundaries for goalies. Hextall is the only goalie, for instance, to have more than 100 penalty minutes in a season. Ron had four children—two boys and two girls—and one of the boys, Brett, was drafted 159th overall by Phoenix at the 2008 Entry Draft. He has yet to play in the NHL, but if he does the Hextalls will be the first family to have four generations of direct descendants in the NHL.

BRANDON SUTTER.

UNBEATABLE
SEASON
RECORDS

THE IMPENETRABLE GEORGE HAINSWORTH

THE RECORD The grand-daddy of all goaltending records, George Hainsworth recorded an incredible twenty-two shutouts in the forty-four game 1928–29 season.

HOW IT WAS DONE Hainsworth took over between the pipes for the Montreal Canadiens starting in 1926 and played almost every minute for the team for the next seven years. He won the Vezina Trophy in each of his first three seasons with the Habs, the last being this historic one in which he recorded twenty-two shutouts, allowed only forty-three goals, and posted a record 0.92 goals-against average.

Despite his outstanding performance, the team won only twenty-two games. Because scoring was low across the league, ties were far more common and the Habs had fifteen of them, including six 0–0 games. The Habs scored only seventy-one goals all year, an average of just 1.61 goals a game. Seven times during the season, Hainsworth had at least two shutouts in a row, once having three and once four in a row. His heroics all season came to nothing in the post-season as the Canadiens were ousted in the first round of the playoffs by Boston, the top team in the

American Division, who were second in goals against that year, allowing only fifty-two.

The Bruins won the best-of-five series in three games by scores of 1–0, 1–0, and 3–2. Goalie Tiny Thompson, who had twelve shutouts in the regular season, outdueled Hainsworth in the playoffs. The Bruins won the Stanley Cup by beating the Rangers in two straight games of a best-of-three Final. The Canadiens, meanwhile, went on to win the Cup in each of the next two years.

WHY IT WON'T BE EQUALLED The 1928–29 season was the last year in which the NHL's original rules were used, primarily those involving passing. Through to this season, forward passing was not allowed. When the rule was dropped the next season, scoring doubled across the league. To illustrate how this affected scoring; Hainsworth allowed forty-three goals and recorded twenty-two shutouts in 1928–29, but he allowed 108 goals and earned only four shutouts the next year. Trying to put Hainsworth's record into a modern context is difficult, but think of a goalie such as Martin Brodeur who plays, say, seventy games a season. He would need to record a shutout every third game to approach twenty-two shutouts, an impossible feat.

SCORING WAY UP

In Hainsworth's record season, not only were teams allowing fewer goals but, of course, teams were scoring fewer. In fact, only Boston, with eighty-nine goals in forty-four games, averaged two goals a game. Every other of the NHL's ten teams scored less than two a game. Compare this to the Edmonton Oilers, who three times averaged well over five goals a game in the 1980s, culminating with 1983–84 when they averaged 5.58 goals per game.

MARTIN BRODEUR HOLDS MOST OF THE SIGNIFICANT CAREER GOALIE RECORDS.

There have been only five goalies who have recorded even close to the number of shutouts Hainsworth had in his record-setting season. And only one of those came after 1929 when forward passing rules were instituted. Hainsworth himself had fourteen in his first full season with Montreal, 1926–27, and three others had fifteen. Alec Connell and Hal Winkler both had fifteen in 1927–28, with Ottawa and Boston, respectively, and Connell also had fifteen in 1925–26 with the Senators.

CHICAGO'S TONY ESPOSITO RECORDED FIFTEEN SHUTOUTS IN HIS ROOKIE SEASON.

IS THIS THE GREATEST SHUTOUT RECORD? In some sense, factoring in eras and rules, the greatest shutout season ever was Tony Esposito's with Chicago in 1969–70. He played sixty-three of the team's seventy-six games, earning a shutout about once every four games. This came at a time when Bobby Orr, Phil Esposito, and the rest of the Boston Bruins were just beginning to set scoring records, but it also came in the years following the NHL's first big expansion. Incredibly, Tony O had two shutouts against four of the Original Six teams (Toronto, Montreal, Boston, Detroit), and seven shutouts against expansion teams (two against Pittsburgh and St. Louis, and one each against Los Angeles, Philadelphia, and Oakland).

But most extraordinary was that he set this record during his rookie season. In fact, before 1969–70 he had all of thirteen NHL games to his credit, all the previous year with Montreal. Perhaps the biggest advantage the newcomer had was that he caught with his right hand, making him a rare breed among goalies and causing confusion for shooters.

MEL HILL'S HAT TRICK OF SUDDEN DEATH THRILLS

THE RECORD In the Bruins–Rangers best-of-seven semi-finals series of 1939, Mel Hill scored three overtime winning goals for the Bruins. No player before or since has done as much in one series.

HOW IT WAS DONE The first game of the series was played on March 21, 1939, and Hill scored in the final minute of the third overtime to give the Bruins a 2–1 win. Speeding down the right wing, he took a perfect pass from Bill Cowley and ripped a high drive over the glove of goalie Dave Kerr with just thirty-five seconds remaining in that sixth period of hockey. The game ended at 1:10 am local time at Madison Square Garden in New York.

The goal was the direct result of brilliant strategy by coach and general manager Art Ross. Cowley centred a line with left winger Roy Conacher and right winger Hill. But Cowley, a right-hand shot, found it preferable to pass to Conacher on the left side. Rangers' coach Lester Patrick always had two men covering Conacher, thus smothering the Bruins' top line. But before the first overtime Ross told Cowley to ignore Conacher and pass to the unguarded Hill. This strategy resulted in a great scoring chance in the first OT and gave the Bruins the winning

MEL HILL (LEFT) AND BILL COWLEY OF THE BRUINS.

MIKE BOSSY OF THE NEW YORK ISLANDERS.

MOST GAME-WINNING GOALS, ONE SERIES
This is another record that cannot possibly be bettered, only tied, but in the 1983 conference finals Mike Bossy scored four game-winning goals in a best-of-seven series against Boston. What makes this slightly less impressive than Hill's accomplishment is that a game-winning goal often comes at an unknown time in the game, unlike an overtime winner. Consider the first game of the Islanders-Bruins series, on April 26, 1983. The Islanders won the game 5–2, and Bossy scored the third New York goal, but it came midway through the second period to give his team a 3–0 lead. Only after the end of the game did this prove to be, in retrospect, the winner.

Boston won game two, but the Islanders took a 2–1 series lead after a 7–3 win. Again, Bossy had the fourth and winning goal, but again it came late in the second period to make the score 4–2. No one knew at the time it would prove to be the winner. Bossy also scored the fourth goal early in the third period of an 8–3 romp in the next game, and in game six he also scored the winner early in the second period of an 8–4 slaughter. The stats show four game winners, but none were, at the time, dramatic. Still, no one before or since has been credited with scoring the game winner of every game in a single playoff series.

RECORDS FOREVER

goal late in the third extra period.

Two nights later, Hill did it again. He scored at 8:24 of the fourth period to give Boston a 3–2 win, beating Bert Gardiner with a shot from the high slot. It was the team's tenth win in a row. The Bruins had jumped to a 2–0 lead with a pair of quick goals late in the first by Conacher and Cowley, but the Rangers got one in the second and then tied it with only 2:14 left in the third thanks to Dutch Hiller. On the winning play, Cowley again made a great rush, got by defenceman Babe Pratt, and dished the puck off to Hill, who let go a shot from forty feet out that beat Gardiner cleanly. The goalie was a surprise starter, taking over for Dave Kerr who couldn't play because of a sore shoulder.

The Bruins won game three by a 4–1 score and had control of the series, but the Blueshirts made a little history of their own, winning the next three games to force a seventh. This marked the first time a series started 3–0 only to be pushed to a deciding game. And in that game, in Boston on April 2, Hill set his record, scoring at 8:00 of the third overtime to give the Bruins a 2–1 win and a 4–3 series victory.

The game ended at 12:40 am on April 3. This time, Hill parked himself at the top of the crease, took a pass from Cowley behind the net, and beat goalie Bert Gardiner with a quick shot, "and in so doing

JOE SAKIC IS THE ALL-TIME LEADER IN PLAYOFF OVER-TIME GOALS.

UNBEATABLE SEASON RECORDS

A small and unspectacular player, Hill was a Manitoban by birth but played his first serious hockey in Saskatoon. He moved on to Sudbury, and after an excellent year in 1936–37, he was signed by the Bruins. He played only a few games in 1937–38, but the next year he was a full-time member of the team and scored ten goals in forty-six games, a decent enough output, though one that certainly didn't anticipate what he would do in his first full playoffs (he had appeared in one previous playoff game in 1938). Hill stayed with the Bruins for four years, played one year during the war with the Brooklyn Americans, and then joined the Leafs in 1943. Over the next four seasons, he had his best offensive years, scoring seventeen goals in 1942–43 and eighteen in 1944–45, the year the Leafs won the Cup. After the war Hill played in the AHL when Toronto's best players returned from duty, and he retired in 1952. He was later inducted into the Manitoba Sports Hall of Fame.

displayed his 'sudden death' virtuosity for the third time during this series," wrote Joseph C. Nichols in the *New York Times*. The Bruins went on to win the Cup, giving Hill his due place in playoff history.

"Bill gave me a perfect pass," Hill described moments after the victory. "I had plenty of time and was in close. Gardiner made the first move, opening his legs, and I just smacked it through. I had to take plenty of time to make it good because I would have been awfully mad with myself if I had missed."

The win against the Rangers was especially sweet for Hill because several years previous he had attended the Rangers' training camp only to be told by Patrick to abandon the sport and go into a profession at which he was qualified. The smart of that remark stayed with Hill.

WHY IT WON'T BE EQUALLED Again, the sheer weight of time is one indicator that this record is safe forever. True, any player, any time in a best-of-seven can tie or even eclipse the record, but in the seventy-one years since, no one has come close. Only once has a player even had three OT goals in a playoff season. Maurice Richard scored twice in OT against Detroit in the 1951 semi-finals and once in the Final against the Leafs. No other player has had more than two in any one year, a fact that makes Hill's record all the more astounding given that the playoffs in the modern era consist of four rounds of best-of-seven. Hill scored only twelve playoff goals in his career, and he never scored another in overtime, but for one memorable spring of hat-trick heroics he earned the nickname "Sudden Death."

CONNIE BRODEN WINS INCREDIBLE DOUBLE

THE RECORD Connie Broden won World Championship gold with Canada in 1958, and just a few weeks later he won the Stanley Cup with the Montreal Canadiens. This double victory will never be replicated.

HOW IT WAS DONE At the start of the 1957–58 season, Broden was hardly a key element of Montreal's plans. He had played three regular season games and six playoff games in previous years—the sum total of his NHL experience—and was playing with the Whitby Dunlops in senior hockey to start the year.

The Dunlops went to Oslo, Norway in March to represent Canada at the World Championship, and Broden had an important role on the team. In fact, he led the Oslo championship in scoring with twelve goals and seven assists in seven games. His most important goal gave Canada a 2–1 lead in the decisive game against the Soviet Union on the final day of the tournament, March 9, 1958. The game ended 4–2 and the Dunlops won Canada its first gold medal in three years.

Just six weeks later, impressed by his showing overseas, the Habs called him up for the playoffs. Broden played only one of the five games in the Stanley Cup Final against Boston, but that was enough

CONNIE BRODEN (RIGHT) WITH A WHITBY DUNLOP TEAMMATE.

BRODEN'S CAREER

Broden's NHL career was as short as it was remarkably successful. In just three seasons with Montreal, he played a mere six NHL games in the regular season and seven more in the playoffs. In all, he recorded only two goals and two assists yet got his name on the Stanley Cup twice, in 1957 and 1958.

to have his name etched on the hallowed trophy as the powerful Habs won for the third straight year. Broden played in game five of the Final, on April 17, 1958, filling in for the injured Floyd Curry. He played mostly as a penalty killer, alternating with Bert Olmstead and Don Marshall.

WHY IT WON'T BE EQUALLED Since 1977, when it was only possible for NHL players whose teams had been eliminated from the Stanley Cup playoffs to play at the World Championships, the double victory has been impossible. Yet, in earlier days when an amateur could turn pro or a pro revert to amateur, no one before or after Broden came close to winning the two great prizes in the same season because such maneuvering was rare. But with the two events running concurrently, it can never be accomplished again.

THE GREATEST INTERNATIONAL ACCOMPLISHMENT? In the long history of international hockey, there have been only five players who have participated in the World Junior (U20) Championship, senior World Championship, and Olympics in the same year. That small group includes Russia's Darius Kasparaitis, Alexei Kovalev, and Alexei Zhitnik, who performed the troika as teammates in 1992, and Saku Koivu of Finland, in 1994.

But most incredible of all was Kenny Jonsson of Sweden. He is the only one to have won a medal at each event (and a different one each time, no less). In 1994, he started the international season by winning silver with the U20 team, then helped Tre Kronor win gold at the Lillehammer Olympics, and finished the season with a bronze at the World Championship. He never did win a Stanley Cup, though, preventing him from joining the Triple Gold Club.

OLYMPIC/STANLEY CUP DOUBLE

Of course, the greater glory is winning Olympic gold and the Stanley Cup. That has happened three times to six players, in 1980, 2002, and 2010. Ken Morrow was the first to accomplish this mighty double, first as a member of the U.S. "Miracle on Ice" team that won gold at Lake Placid in February 1980, and then in May that year, winning the Cup with the New York Islanders. In 2002, Canada won gold in Salt Lake and the Detroit Red Wings won the Stanley Cup. Brendan Shanahan and Steve Yzerman were members of both teams. In 2010, Jonathan Toews, Brent Seabrook, and Duncan Keith were all members of Canada's Olympic win in Vancouver and Chicago's Cup triumph.

TOP: (L-R) BRENT SEABROOK, JONATHAN TOEWS, AND DUNCAN KEITH CELEBRATED OLYMPIC GOLD IN FEBRUARY 2010 AND THEN WON THE CUP THAT SAME JUNE.

BOTTOM: TOEWS WON THE CUP WITH CHICAGO JUST A FEW MONTHS AFTER WINNING OLYMPIC GOLD.

HARVEY COACHES RANGERS AND WINS NORRIS—IN THE SAME YEAR

THE RECORD Defenceman Doug Harvey made history in two ways. First, he is the only player to win an individual trophy in consecutive years with different teams, and second, he is also the only player to win an individual trophy while coaching a team.

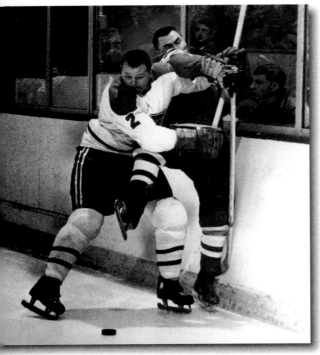

HARVEY SQUISHES AN OPPONENT OUT OF THE PLAY.

HOW IT WAS DONE Anyone who saw Doug Harvey play said he was the precursor to Bobby Orr. He could rush the puck and control the play, and when he was on the ice he was like a general, able to alter the rhythm and pace of the game, and able to change the outcome. A gifted skater, he could carry the puck up ice like no one else, and he led the offence when the puck was inside enemy territory.

But after thirteen years, the Habs believed his best days were behind him and his work in trying to unionize the players deserved punishment, so they traded him to the lowly Rangers in the summer of 1961 for nothing more than fighter Lou Fontinato. Harvey had just won the Norris Trophy for the sixth time, and when he got to New York he was also named coach. Harvey, with much to prove, had a sensational season on the blue-line and behind the bench, leading the team to the playoffs and winning the Norris Trophy again. He was aided in changing lines at the bench by Muzz Patrick, but it was Harvey who directed the team in all manners of performance.

In his first game with the Rangers, a 6–2 win at the Boston Garden, Harvey showed what he could do. He scored in the second period to give the Blueshirts a 2–1 lead while on the power play, and he was outstanding in his own end as well.

WHY IT WON'T BE EQUALLED

It is no longer permitted for a team to have a playing coach, so a coach winning an individual honour for his play on ice is simply out of the question. As for winning a trophy in consecutive years with two different teams, well, it's possible, of course, but since it's been done only once—and that by one of the greatest players in the game's history—it isn't likely to happen

NOT EVEN GRETZKY? Even the Great One had a break during his many wins of the Art Ross and Hart Trophies when he was traded from Edmonton to Los Angeles in 1988. He won the scoring title for seven straight years (1981–88), but then didn't win it his first two years in L.A. before winning three more times with the Kings in a five-year span. Ditto for the Hart Trophy. He won eight in a row with the Oilers, lost in 1987–88 to Mario Lemieux, and won with the Kings the next year. He is, however, one of only two players to win the Art Ross with different teams, the other player being Joe Malone who won with the Canadiens in the NHL's inaugural season of 1917–18, and two years later with the Quebec Bulldogs. Gretzky and Red Kelly are also the only players to win the Lady Byng Trophy with two teams. In 99's case, it was Edmonton and Los Angeles, of course, and for Kelly it was Detroit and Toronto.

JACK ADAMS

Although there have been several multiple winners of coach of the year, there is only one coach who won the award with the same team in consecutive years. Jacques Demers won it with Detroit in both 1986–87 and 1987–88. This is an anomaly because the award generally acknowledges some drastic improvement of the team. In the first year, Demers nearly doubled the Red Wings' point output over the previous year, going from forty to seventy-eight. In the second year, he took the team to the top of the Norris Division, meriting, in voters' eyes, a second Adams Award. Pat Burns has the distinction of winning coach of the year honours three times with three different Original Six teams—Montreal in 1989, Toronto in 1993, and Boston in 1998.

again. No player has won the Art Ross Trophy in consecutive years with different teams, not even Wayne Gretzky when he went from Edmonton to Los Angeles in 1988. Ditto for the Hart Trophy or any other of the important individual awards.

COACH PAT BURNS ENLIVENS THE TORONTO BENCH.

JOE THORNTON WON THE ART ROSS AND HART TROPHIES IN A YEAR HE WAS TRADED.

SILVERWARE TWO-TIMERS The awarding and winning of hockey's silverware has traditionally been symbolic of the finest players playing their finest for a full season. In all the years the many trophies have been awarded, the number of anomalies can be counted on one hand. For instance, only once has a player won the Art Ross or Hart Trophy in a year in which he played for two teams.

In 2005–06, Boston traded Joe Thornton to the San Jose Sharks, and Thornton went on to win the scoring race and later the Hart Trophy. This marked the only time these trophies have been given out to a player who was traded mid-season. No goalie has ever been traded and won the William Jennings Trophy, and only once has a traded player won the Lady Byng. Jean Ratelle had that honour in 1975–76 when he was traded from the Rangers to the Bruins. As well, no player has won the Calder Trophy or Lester B. Pearson/Ted Lindsay Award during a season in which he was traded.

HOWE DOES GORDIE GET 103 POINTS AT AGE FORTY?

THE RECORD Only one time in twenty-six years of his NHL career did the great Gordie Howe ever reach the 100-point mark. That came in 1968–69, when he amassed 103 points in the seventy-six-game season. He was a day shy of his forty-first birthday.

HOW IT WAS DONE Despite being forty in his twenty-third NHL season, Howe had a remarkable year. He played every game of the seventy-six-game schedule, had points in twenty-three of the team's first twenty-five games, including a four-point night against the Rangers on December 8 (two goals, two assists), and four games of three points. On December 4, 1968, against Pittsburgh, he scored his 700th career goal. In February, he had hat-trick games just ten days apart, and he had six game-winning goals on the season. He also finished with a plus-45 rating, making him one of the top plus-minus leaders in the league.

Coming into the Chicago Stadium on March 30, 1969, for the final game of the regular season, Gordie Howe knew history could be made. His Detroit Red Wings were set to play Chicago, and he had forty-two goals and fifty-seven assists for ninety-nine points. All he wanted was one more goal or assist to reach the century mark. He got four. Gordie scored twice in the second period and added two assists in the final period, and although the Black Hawks won the game, 9–5, Gordie became just the third player in history to reach the century mark as well as the oldest. Some forty-two years later, he is still the oldest to reach the milestone. Just a couple of hours after that final game, he turned forty-one. More notably, he hit the forty-goal mark for the first time in twelve years and broke the league record for most points and assists by a right winger.

FIRST TO 100

Howe was the third player to hit the 100-point mark in NHL history, all coming in 1968–69. Before him came Phil Esposito, who had 126, and Bobby Hull, who had 107. That all three reached the mark in the same month—the first time anyone in NHL history had hit 100—is also remarkable testament to how difficult an achievement it was. Espo connected on March 2, Hull on March 20, and Howe ten days later. All got their 100th points on goals. Esposito was twenty-seven years old at the time and Hull was thirty.

HOWE SCORED HIS 700TH CAREER GOAL ON DECEMBER 4, 1968, BY BEATING PITTSBURGH'S LES BINKLEY WITH A SHOT.

GRETZKY'S FINAL NHL GOAL ALSO LEFT NO DOUBT WHO WAS THE GREATEST SCORER IN HOCKEY HISTORY.

LAST SEASONS OF THE GREATS Wayne Gretzky's final season was 1998–99. The all-time scoring leader had sixty-two points in his last season at age thirty-eight. Steve Yzerman's last season was 2005–06. He had thirty-four points in sixty-one games at age forty. Phil Esposito's last full season was 1979–80 with the Rangers. He had seventy-eight points at age thirty-eight, then played part of another season and retired.

The loss of touch, speed, and skill is inevitable, and for a forty-year-old just to be in the NHL and play a full season is rare. In 2010–11, Mark Recchi ended the season as a forty-three-year-old, the oldest player in the league. He played eighty-one games and was an impressive plus-13 with the Bruins. He had forty-eight points, less than half Howe's total. The forty-year-old Teemu Selanne had an incredible season in 2010–11, scoring eighty points with the Ducks, including thirty-one goals, but still way behind Howe's output.

WHY IT WON'T BE EQUALLED

In 2010–11, there was one player who hit the 100-point mark, Daniel Sedin of Vancouver, who had 104. The year before that there were four, and the year before that, three. Getting 100 points was a rare achievement in Howe's day, and it is almost as rare today. Coupled with that, the NHL has gotten immeasurably younger. In 2010–11, there were just three forty-year-olds, Mark Recchi (Boston), Teemu Selanne (Anaheim), and Dwayne Roloson (Tampa Bay). Just to play in the NHL at forty is extraordinary, and scoring 100 points, even at a young age, is as rare. To find a player who can do both is virtually impossible.

NEXT OLDEST

Gretzky's last 100-point season came with Los Angeles in 1993–94 when he had 130. He was thirty-three years old. Lemieux was thirty-one when he had his last century season, with the Penguins in 1996–97. Esposito was also thirty-three when he had 127 points with the Bruins in 1974–75, his last 100-plus season. The next most impressive season was surely Johnny Bucyk who had 116 points for Boston in 1970–71 when he was thirty-five. Players peak around age twenty-four and continue to produce great offence into their early thirties. But forty-year-olds are lucky to survive, let alone thrive. Howe stands alone as a 100-point-scoring quadragenarian.

JOHNNY BUCYK (RIGHT) REACHED 100 POINTS IN A SEASON AT AGE THIRTY-FIVE.

MIKKELSON'S GREAT GOLF SCORE A HOCKEY HORROR

THE RECORD Playing for the hapless Washington Capitals in 1974–75, defenceman Bill Mikkelson accrued a plus-minus of minus-82 in just fifty-nine games before being sent down to the minors. This is the worst plus-minus for a season in NHL history.

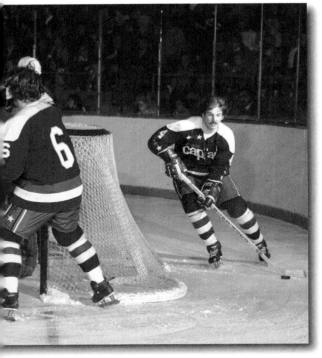

HOW IT WAS DONE The Washington Capitals were the worst of the worst. In 1974–75, the team posted a record of 8–67–5. They scored only 181 goals and surrendered 446, losing games by an average of three and a half goals (5.58-2.26). They won only one road game all year (in forty games), that coming in game number seventy-five of an eighty-game schedule and their thirty-eighth of forty road games. The Caps never won two games in a row and once lost seventeen straight. They also had winless streaks during the season of fourteen and nine games. The team had three coaches—Jim Anderson, Red Sullivan, and Milt Schmidt—and goalie Michel Belhumeur had a season record of 0–24–3, the most losses ever posted in a season without a single victory.

Although the Caps lost their first game, 6–3, to the Rangers, Mikkelson was a plus-1 on this night, on for two goals for and one even strength against. He wasn't so lucky in the next game, a 6–0 loss to Minnesota in which he was a minus-3. He was minus-1 in the next game against Chicago and followed with a minus-2 against Detroit. After being a healthy scratch for three games, he was a plus-1 against Toronto, a 4–3 loss, but was a minus-2 against Buffalo next game.

And so the season went. Mikkelson was a "plus player" only nine times. He had a season high plus-2 just twice, October 17 and November 19, and was a plus-1 on seven occasions.

He had three notably disastrous outings. On December 7, 14, and 29, he was a minus-5 each time. For the most part, though, his plus-minus sunk further and further in trickles. He would often be a minus-1 or minus-2 in a game, and, of course, the Caps lost almost every game they played, giving him and the rest of the beleaguered defensive corps little time to recover or enjoy a night of victory, let alone an unbeaten streak.

By month, he was minus-4 in October, minus-15 in November, minus-27 in December, minus-13 in January, and minus-23 in February. He missed two games at the end of February and was then sold to Los Angeles on March 3, 1975, in a simple cash transaction.

CAREER

Mikkelson is not as hapless as the numbers might suggest. He was signed by Los Angeles in 1970 and spent two years in the Kings' system. This included a fifteen-game callup in 1971–72, his first NHL experience. He was claimed by the expansion New York Islanders in the summer of 1972 and posted a minus-54 in seventy-two games with a terrible team that won just twelve of seventy-eight games and gave up 347 goals (an average of 4.45 per game). He spent all of the next season in the minors, but again in the summer of 1974 he was claimed by the Caps in the Expansion Draft before embarking on his season of infamy. After this disastrous 1974–75 outing, he played just one more NHL game and retired altogether in 1977.

WHAT IS PLUS-MINUS? Pundits agree this is hardly a universally accepted statistic of merit. It is calculated by recording which players are on ice for goals scored and goals allowed, but there is one exception. While short-handed goals count in plus-minus stats, power-play goals do not, the theory being that a team that allows a shorty should be given a minus while scoring a goal while a man down deserves credit. But, to count a power-play goal to plus-minus stats would be unfair to the penalized team and an unjust reward to the scoring team (given the manpower advantage). So, a player who is on the ice for 100 goals scored by his team and ninety goals scored by the opposition has a plus/minus score of plus-10. But if all of those goals came during the power play, his plus-minus would be, simply, zero.

WASHINGTON
capitals™

FAMILY

The Mikkelson lineage is impressive. Bill's uncle was Jim McFadden, who was a Calder Cup trophy winner with Chicago in 1948 and Stanley Cup winner with Detroit in 1950. Bill's son, Brendan, was drafted by Anaheim in 2005, and his daughter Meaghan has had an outstanding (and ongoing) career with Canada's national women's team, culminating with Olympic gold in Vancouver 2010.

WHY IT WON'T BE EQUALLED

Mikkelson's record has been safe for thirty-seven years and will never be broken because the NHL has implemented rules to create parity such that no team will ever win just eight games in eighty ever again. The league has also expanded to such a degree that further expansion is unlikely, so teams will never have such a weak season as expansion teams typically do. Also, a player with such a terrible plus-minus will not be put in the lineup to play fifty-nine games for the team. There are too many minor leaguers waiting for a chance to prove themselves who can do better than minus-82.

CANADA'S MEAGHAN MIKKELSON
WON OLYMPIC GOLD IN 2010.

NOT ALONE Yes, Mikkelson's minus-82 remains a record that won't be beat, but he was hardly alone on that 1974–75 Washington team. Consider that teammate Greg Joly posted a minus-68 in just forty-four games. Gord Smith was minus-56 in sixty-three games, Yvon Labre was minus-54 in seventy-six games, and Doug Mohns was a minus-52 in seventy-five games. Labre had his number 7 retired by the Caps and Mohns was in his final season of a twenty-two-year, 1,390-game career. Mikkelson was merely the defenceman with the worst number on a team infamous for its poor play all season long.

BOBBY ORR WINS THE ART ROSS TROPHY— TWICE

THE RECORD The greatest defenceman in the history of the game, Bobby Orr twice won the NHL's scoring championship, a feat that no other blue-liner has ever even remotely approached.

HOW IT WAS DONE When Bobby Orr joined the NHL, the game changed. Orr was a rushing defenceman who not only brought the puck out of his own end, he would go the full length of the ice with the puck, forcing defenders to cope with a fourth forward. He was the game's strongest skater and best stickhandler as well. Within a couple of years, the Bruins had built a team with incredible offensive force, and a goalie, Gerry Cheevers, who could stop shots when it mattered most.

In 1969–70, Orr was twenty-one years old and in his prime. He obliterated records for most goals by a defenceman (33), and most assists by any player (87). His 120 total points was far and away the most in the league. Second was teammate and forward Phil Esposito, who had ninety-nine points. Winning the scoring title by twenty-one points was also the greatest margin of victory in NHL history, a margin that wasn't bettered until Esposito won by twenty-six points in 1972–73. Orr won the Art Ross Trophy again in 1974–75 with 135 points, eight more than Espo.

INJURIES, AS MUCH AS GOALS AND ASSISTS,
CAME TO DEFINE ORR'S CAREER.

ORR'S SHORTENED CAREER

Although the records show that Orr retired early in the 1978–79 season at age thirty, his last full season was in 1974–75. He played only nine full seasons and recorded 100 points six straight years, but he missed games and then years because of serious knee injuries. Still, he had 915 career points in only 657 games and left a mark on the ice that goes well beyond mere numbers and statistical records.

In 1969–70, Orr had one five-point game (all assists, December 20 against Pittsburgh), five four-point games, and twelve three-point games. His longest point-less streak was all of two games.

Incredibly, neither of his Art Ross seasons was Orr's best statistically. In 1970–71, he had 139 points, still the most in a season by a defenceman, but Esposito led the league with 152. It was also at

ORR (LEFT) POSES WITH THIRD GOALIE ED JOHNSTON PRIOR TO THE 1972 SUMMIT SERIES.

THE ORR FILE

In addition to his two Art Ross Trophies, Orr won the Calder Trophy in his rookie season and the Hart Trophy three times. He won the Lester B. Pearson Award in 1974–75 and the Norris Trophy an unprecedented eight straight years. Orr is also one of only five players to have scored two Stanley Cup-winning goals (along with Jack Darragh, Henri Richard, Mike Bossy, and Jacques Lemaire) and twice won the Conn Smythe Trophy as a result. He was also named tournament MVP of the 1976 Canada Cup, the only international event he played, despite having only one good knee to skate on by that point in his career.

this time that the Bruins did something that had never been done before, has never been done since, and will never be done at any time in the future—they placed the top four scorers in both 1970–71 and 1973–74. In the former, Esposito and Orr were followed by Johnny Bucyk (116) and Ken Hodge (105). Doubly amazing, these four were the only ones to reach the 100-point mark in the league. In 1973–74, Espo was first with 145 and Orr second again with 122. Then followed Espo's linemates, Hodge (with 105) and Wayne Cashman (89).

The first team with the top three scorers was Boston in 1939–40 (the line of Milt Schmidt, Woody Dumart, and Bobby Bauer placing 1–2–3). Three times after it was done, twice by Montreal (1944–45 and 1954–55) and once by Detroit, (1949–50). Since Boston's top-four record, no team has even placed the top three scorers. That Orr was among this quartet on both occasions, in years he didn't win the Art Ross Trophy, is simply extraordinary.

WHY IT WON'T BE EQUALLED Orr ushered in an era of unprecedented offence from the blue-line. His rushing style created havoc for the defending team and gave coaches headaches trying to stop a puck carrier who came from behind the play rather than in front. However, coaches have since stressed defence first, and a rushing defenceman is now considered irresponsible. Team defence is also much better and more determined, and interference in the form of hooking and slashing is such that going end-to-end is almost impossible. As well, of course, just as there was only one Gretzky, there was only one Orr. No defenceman before him came close to winning the Art Ross, and no one since has threatened to do what he did.

PAUL COFFEY.

SECOND BEST For all the great rushing defencemen who followed, from Brad Park to Denis Potvin, Larry Robinson to Paul Coffey, no one came close to winning the scoring title. Coffey produced incredible numbers, but he was always way behind teammate Wayne Gretzky, who smashed virtually every scoring record there was. In 1983–84, for instance, Coffey was second in league scoring with 126 points, but Gretzky was seventy-nine points ahead with 205. The top-scoring defenceman in 2010–11 was Washington's Mike Green, and his seventy-six points placed him in a tie for twentieth overall, well behind Henrik Sedin of Vancouver, who won the scoring title with 112 points. The last time a defenceman was even in the top-ten of scoring was Coffey, in 1994–95, the lockout-shortened season. He had fifty-eight points, tied for sixth.

HABS LOSE JUST EIGHT GAMES IN A SEASON

THE RECORD In 1976–77, the Montreal Canadiens had a record of 60–8–12 in eighty games, the fewest losses ever in a season of comparable length. In the playoffs, they won twelve and lost only two more games, giving them a total of just ten losses in ninety-two games. They won the Stanley Cup.

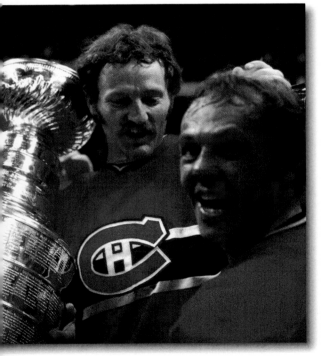

LARRY ROBINSON (LEFT) CELEBRATES CUP VICTORY WITH YVAN COURNOYER.

HOW IT WAS DONE With a team of nine future Hall of Famers, the Canadiens started their 1976–77 season at home with a 10–1 slaughter of Pittsburgh. They lost their third and seventh games, but over the course of the next thirteen games, they lost only once. Then, between late November and early January, they went another twenty-one games with only a single loss. In mid-January, they actually lost twice in a three-game span, but then Scotty Bowman coached the team to a twenty-one-game unbeaten streak which included seventeen wins and four ties. After a loss to Buffalo, the Habs closed out the season with another twelve-game unbeaten streak.

In the playoffs, they swept St. Louis, beat the Islanders 4–2 in the best-of-seven, and finished the year with a four-game sweep of Boston to win their second straight Stanley Cup. To put the record into perspective, the last time a team lost only eight games in a season was the Canadiens, in 1944–45, when teams played a fifty-game schedule.

Guy Lafleur led all scorers that year with 136 points while teammate Steve Shutt led all goalscorers with sixty (Lafleur was second with fifty-six). At the other end, Larry Robinson led all defencemen with eighty-five points, and goalie Ken Dryden posted ridiculously impressive numbers—fifty-six games played, with a record of 41–6–8, which included ten shutouts, and a 2.14 goals-against average. He and backup Michel Larocque shared the Vezina Trophy by allowing a combined 171 goals all year.

In all, some fourteen players on the team had at least thirteen goals, and Doug Risebrough was far and away the most penalized player with 132 PIMs (second on the team was Mario Tremblay with just sixty-one). The days of the Broad Street Bullies were over, and Montreal's firewagon hockey was in full force.

WHO BEAT THE HABS?

The eight losses came as follows:

1–October 10, 1976	Montreal 1 at Buffalo 3		5–December 12, 1976	Montreal 2 at NY Rangers 5
2–October 17, 1976	Montreal 3 at Boston 5		6–January 12, 1977	Montreal 2 at St. Louis 7
3–October 30, 1976	Boston 4 at Montreal 3		7–January 17, 1977	Montreal 3 at Boston 7
4–November 17, 1976	Montreal 0 at Toronto 1		8–March 6, 1977	Montreal 1 at Buffalo 4

Notice that the team lost only once at home and was shut out only once all year. Boston accounted for three of those losses and Buffalo two. These were among the top five teams in the league this year, and it was the Bruins whom Montreal hammered in four straight games of the Cup Final to win the championship.

GOAL DIFFERENTIAL

That 1976–77 season saw Montreal score 387 goals and surrender only 171, a goal differential of 216. This is also the best of all time. The Bruins team of 1970–71 was a plus-182, and the Montreal team of 1975–76 was a plus-176. The high-scoring Edmonton Oilers' best season as far as goal differential was 1983–84 when they were a plus-132, and even that sensational Detroit team with 131 points in 1995–96 was only a plus-144. With the drop in goalscoring in recent decades, a greater differential has been impossible to achieve. There must be a fine balance between plenty of offence but the possibility of good defence. If the entire league is defensively-oriented, it's not possible to score enough goals to create a huge enough goal differential. Indeed, that plus-216 for the Habs is the third record from that season which isn't likely to be bettered.

WHY IT WON'T BE EQUALLED

Of course, unless a team has a record of 82–0–0 it can't call itself perfect, but this 1976–77 season is as close to perfection as a hockey team can get. Given the length of the schedule, the travel, the number of teams in the league, and competitive balance, a team cannot possibly play at such a high level for the entire season. The Habs recorded 132 points in the standings that year, another record that has proved untouchable. More important, Montreal continued to do in the playoffs what it had done all season and won the Stanley Cup.

GOALIE KEN DRYDEN WAS ALMOST UNBEATABLE ALL SEASON.

THE HABS CONTINUED THEIR GREAT PLAY THROUGH THE
PLAYOFFS, WINNING THE CUP IN THE SPRING OF 1977.

CLOSE, BUT NO CIGAR From 1976–77 to the present the league has gone from eighteen teams to thirty, but expansion hasn't watered the league down so much as allowed more Europeans a chance to play. Consider that the Habs had 132 points in the standings during its record year. Only five other times in NHL history has a team had even 120 points. Boston, in 1970–71, had 121, but lost fourteen games that year in a seventy-eight-game season.

In 1972–73 the Habs had 120 points, and lost ten games in a seventy-eight-game schedule. In 1975–76, the Habs improved to 127 points and eleven losses when teams played eighty games. The only other 120 points-or-more seasons belong to Detroit. The Red Wings nearly tied the Habs in 1995–96 when they had 131, but they lost thirteen times in an eighty-two-game season. In 2005–06, the Wings had 124 points in a sixteen-loss season. All great seasons, but those eight losses remain an incredible achievement. Interestingly, both Detroit teams and the early Boston team failed to win the Cup, but all three Montreal teams on this list did go on to win.

FLYERS GO THIRTY-FIVE GAMES WITHOUT A LOSS

THE RECORD The Philadelphia Flyers started their 1979–80 season with a standard-issue, 5–2 win at home against the New York Islanders. Two nights later, in Atlanta, the Flames hammered them 9–2. Philadelphia then went on a thirty-five-game unbeaten streak, not losing again until January 7, 1980.

HOW IT WAS DONE Coached by Pat Quinn, the Flyers of 1979–80 still had several players from its brawling, Cup-winning teams of the mid-1970s, notably, captain Bobby Clarke and right winger Reggie Leach, as well as Bill Barber and Rick MacLeish. They beat Toronto by a 4–3 score on October 14 to begin the streak and followed with easy wins over Atlanta (6–2) and Detroit (7–3). The next game was a 6–6 tie, a game that never should have been so close. The Flyers led 6–2 midway through the second period but took victory for granted. The Habs scored twice near the end of the period to cut the margin to two, and they got the only two goals of the third to tie the game, the final goal coming from Rejean Houle at 17:11.

Two games later, the Flyers got a late goal to break a 4–4 tie and beat the Red Wings, and on November 7, they rallied from an early 2–0 deficit to beat the Quebec Nordiques, 4–3. Ten days later, St. Louis held a 2–0 lead after two periods, but the Flyers rallied and tied the game, 3–3. On December 4, Boston held a 2–0 lead in the second period, but again the Flyers fought back for a 2–2 tie.

One of their closest games came on December 20, against Pittsburgh. Ron Stackhouse scored midway through the first period for the Pens. The goal stood up for most of the game until the Flyers tied the score on the power play at 15:52 of the third period. Defenceman

THE STREAK MEANT NOTHING IN THE PLAYOFFS

The Flyers rode that streak to first place overall that year, finishing with twelve losses and 116 points. However, they fell just short in the playoffs. They swept Edmonton in the first round, best-of-five, then beat the Rangers and North Stars in five games each to advance to the Cup Final, but the Islanders were better and won the Cup in six games.

(L-R) FLYERS ANDRE DUPONT, BOBBY CLARKE, AND REGGIE LEACH HELPED THE TEAM TO THIRTY-FIVE GAMES WITHOUT A LOSS.

BILL BARBER.

Behn Wilson scored the goal to keep the streak alive at twenty-eight games. That was as close as the team came to losing. Incredibly, there was no game with a last-second goal, goalie on the bench, streak almost over situation. The Flyers were in control of most games and were simply the better and more motivated team every night.

Then, on January 7, in Minnesota, they got the early goal to lead 1–0, but the North Stars scored three before the end of the period, added two more in the second, and added a final two in the third to crush the Flyers 7–1 and end the streak at thrity-five games.

WHY IT WON'T BE EQUALLED To go half a season and nearly three months without a loss is unheard of, and in this day and age of scouting and systems, video and detailed preparation, it is not possible for a team to play thirty-five NHL games without a loss. The next longest streak was twenty-eight, by Montreal in 1977–78. Not only is the Flyers' streak an NHL record, but no team in any other sport in North America has bettered this record either.

OTHER WIN STREAKS The Los Angeles Lakers of the NBA had a streak of thirty-three wins in a row during the 1971–72 season. Because there are no ties in basketball, this might be a purer record than the Flyers, who had ten ties to go with their twenty-five wins. The New York Giants in baseball had a twenty-six-game unbeaten streak in 1916 (which included a tie). The Indianapolis Colts of the NFL won twenty-three games in a row (2008–09), while the Calgary Stampeders went twenty-two games in a row without losing (1948–49) in CFL play.

RECORDS FOREVER

COACH PAT QUINN

A life in hockey gave Quinn many great memories, but never a Stanley Cup. He got back to the Final only one other time, in 1994 with Vancouver, but the Canucks lost to the Rangers in game seven. Quinn coached exactly 1,400 regular-season games, winning 684. He led Canada to Olympic gold in 2002 and to the championship of the World Cup of Hockey in 2004. He also took Canada's U18 team to gold in 2008 and the U20 team to gold in 2009.

COACH PAT QUINN WAS THE GUIDING FORCE BEHIND THE BENCH FOR THE FLYERS.

GORDIE HOWE PLAYS WITH HIS SONS— AT AGE FIFTY-TWO

THE RECORD Gordie Howe played the full eighty games of the 1979–80 NHL season with the Hartford Whalers. It was his twenty-sixth NHL season and thirty-second pro season. It also marked the only time a father played an NHL game with his sons. Gordie was fifty-one at the start of the season and fifty-two by the time he played his last game. Howe's first NHL season was 1946–47.

GORDIE HOWE (RIGHT) WITH SON, MARK.

HOW IT WAS DONE When Gordie Howe retired from the NHL in 1971, after a quarter of a century with the Detroit Red Wings, he was done. Arthritic in both wrists and forty-three years old, the all-time leading scorer with 1,809 points had done it all. But when the WHA started in 1972, and the owners of the Houston Aeros called him the following summer, he reconsidered retirement. Why? They offered him a chance to play with his sons, Mark and Marty. The three jumped at the opportunity and played together throughout that 1973–74 season in the WHA.

Incredibly, Gordie had thirty-one goals and 100 points that year and was named the league's MVP. He was forty-six years old. The three Howes spent the next six years together playing as a family, first with the Aeros and then, starting in 1977, with the New England Whalers. In the summer of 1979, the WHA merged with the NHL and the Howes decided to keep going when the team (renamed the Hartford Whalers) was one of four to join the NHL.

Gordie was kept by the Whalers during the transition while Mark was claimed by Boston and then re-claimed by the Whalers in the Priority Draft. Marty had his rights retained by the Whalers and didn't have to be exposed in the Expansion Draft. As a result, all three Howes were able to join the NHL Whalers without difficulty.

On October 11, 1979, the Hartford Whalers played their inaugural NHL game on the road against Minnesota, and Gordie took the ice with his son Mark to become the first father to play with his son in the NHL. Marty, his other son, was in the minors much of the year and played just six games with the Whalers. Mark missed several games due to an injury, so the only time all three Howes played

OTHER GOLDEN OLDIES

The only other two NHLers who played to an age close to Howe's were goalie Johnny Bower and defenceman Chris Chelios. Bower last played with the Leafs on December 10, 1969, at age forty-five, while Chelios's last game was April 6, 2010, as a member of the Atlanta Thrashers. He was forty-eight.

BOBBY HULL (LEFT) WITH THE ELDER GORDIE HOWE.

The oldest NBA player was Nat Hickey, who played for the Providence Steam-rollers in 1948 at age forty-five (two days before his forty-sixth birthday, in fact). The oldest Major League Baseball player was Satchel Paige, who pitched in the majors at age fifty-eight. Given the lack of conditioning or physical contact needed to play the game, this is hardly as impressive as Howe's achievement. Paige pitched only three innings, and his last previous full-time duty in MLB was twelve years earlier. Quarterback George Blanda played for the Oakland Raiders in the NFL at age forty-eight in 1975.

together was four games—March 9, 12, 13, and 19. Gordie played seventy-four games with one son, and four games with two sons, a nearly incomprehensible achievement.

WHY IT WON'T BE EQUALLED In one all-encompassing sentence: This record won't be beat because there is only one Gordie Howe. His longevity—and consistently high performance—defy logic, defy time, defy the mortality of pro athletes. No competitor in such a physically-demanding sport has played at age fifty-two. But for the sake of argument, how could someone accomplish what Howe did? First, a player would have to make the NHL. Then, he'd have to get married and have two sons at a young age. Then, both boys would have to go on to be exceptional hockey players such that they could play in the NHL. And, finally, the father would have to play at least twenty years in the NHL in order to have the chance to play with his sons. More than 7,000 players in a century of the NHL have passed through the league, and only one has played beyond even his forty-eighth birthday. His name is Gordie Howe.

THE HISTORIC SEASON OF 1979–80 Of course, 1967 is a pivotal year in NHL history because the league expanded from six to twelve teams that summer. But one might easily argue that the birth of the modern game came in 1979, when the four WHA teams joined the NHL—Edmonton, Winnipeg, Hartford, and Quebec. The Amateur Draft became the Entry Draft and eighteen-year-olds were now eligible. And Wayne Gretzky began his NHL career.

Gretzky's idol as a boy was Gordie Howe, and number 99 realized a dream on December 9, 1979, when the two played against each other, in Edmonton. Gretzky had a goal and assist, and the Oilers won, 3–0.

(L-R) MARK HOWE, GORDIE HOWE, AND NICK FOTIU HOP OVER THE BOARDS.

HOWE'S SEASON What makes Howe's final NHL season so memorable was that there was nothing gratuitous about his participation. He played all eighty games, one of only four players on the team to do so. (Mark played seventy-four and Marty broke his arm and missed most of the rest of the season after playing the first six games.) Gordie also scored fifteen goals and forty-one points, tied with Al Sims for seventh in team scoring. He was a plus-9, a very respectable number that clearly indicated he wasn't a liability when on the ice. In the playoffs, the Canadiens swept Hartford in three games of the best-of-five, but Howe had a goal and assist in the series even though the Whalers scored just eight goals in total.

FIFTY GOALS IN FIFTY GAMES? TRY FIFTY IN THIRTY-NINE

THE RECORD On December 30, 1981, Wayne Gretzky scored his fiftieth goal of the season in just his thirty-ninth game.

GRETZKY SCORES ONE OF HIS FIVE GOALS TO REACH FIFTY IN THIRTY-NINE GAMES.

HOW IT WAS DONE The 1981–82 season promised a great deal before it began. Wayne Gretzky had entered the league two years earlier and tied Marcel Dionne for the league lead with 137 points, losing the Art Ross Trophy only because Dionne had more goals (53 to 51). No matter. In Gretzky's second year he set the all-time single season record with 164 points, signaling a new era of offence unlike any previously witnessed. Ironically, though, Gretzky was held to a single assist in his first two games of 1981–82, a 7–4 win over Colorado and a 6–2 loss to Vancouver.

He then went on a nice little run, scoring seven goals in his next eight games, and after a goalless game against the Islanders, he had a little explosion, scoring twice against the Rangers, four times against Quebec, and twice again against Toronto to start November. Now, Gretzky had fifteen goals in his first fourteen games. In the thirteen games he played that month, he had eighteen goals, and it was clear he was on pace for at least fifty goals in fifty games.

This was a magic target, first reached by Maurice Richard in 1944–45 and not equaled until Mike Bossy did it in 1980–81.

December started with a goal drought that threatened the record, as Gretzky went four games without scoring. The final push towards immortality began on December 9 against Los Angeles. Entering the game, he had thirty-one goals in thirty games. He had a goal in each of his next four games, to make it thirty-five in thirty-four, and then Gretzky simply went berserk. He scored a hat trick against Minnesota (38 in 35), twice against Calgary (40 in 36), once against Vancouver (41 in 37), four times against the Kings (45 in 38), and then five times against the Flyers, the last, into an empty net, giving him fifty goals in just thirty-nine games from the start of the season.

The final five goals were typical of how Gretzky scored—that is, every which way. He didn't have the one-timer down pat like Brett Hull; he didn't fire in the slot like Phil Esposito; he didn't barrel down the wing like Guy Lafleur. But Gretzky could put the puck in from anywhere.

FIFTY IN FIFTY

Maurice Richard set the standard for goalscoring when he scored fifty times in the fifty-game-1944–45 season. It was thirty-six years before anyone did it again, and it has been done only seven times since then. Mike Bossy was the first to do it after Richard, scoring his fiftieth goal in the final minutes of his fiftieth game against Quebec in 1981, and Brett Hull did it twice, once in his fiftieth game, once in his forty-ninth. Mario Lemieux had fifty in forty-six games, and Gretzky did it three times, the first his all-time fifty in thirty-nine. In 1983–84, he did it in forty-two games, and the next year he did it in forty-nine games. Fifty in fifty? Too slow for the Great One.

MAURICE RICHARD IS HAULED TO THE ICE BY THE BOSTON PAIR OF JERRY TOPPAZZINI (LEFT) AND LEO BOIVIN.

Another Gretzky record that doesn't get the same attention as his fifty-in-thirty-nine or some of his other incredible achievements is what he did to start the 1983–84 season. Gretzky scored his 100th point of that season in just his thirty-fourth game. Indeed, a player has reached 100 points before the fortieth game only five times, and Gretzky has done it four of those. The only other player who did it was Mario Lemieux, who reached 100 in thirty-eight games to start the 1988–89 season. But for Gretzky to average close to three points a game for half a season is beyond extraordinary. Daniel Sedin was the only 100-point man in the NHL in 2010–11, and it took him the full season to get there.

His first goal of the night, and forty-sixth of the season, came after a carom off the back boards from a Paul Coffey point shot. Number forty-seven was a slapshot from the faceoff circle that surprised goalie Pete Peeters due to its speed and location. Number forty-eight was another slapshot, this time on a break-away, beating Peeters stickside. Number forty-nine, in the third period, came after he deked defenceman Bob Hoffmeyer out of his jock and ripped a quick shot over Peeters' glove again. The fiftieth came at 19:57 into an empty Flyers net, Bill Barber diving in vain at his blue-line to prevent Gretzky from hitting the net. Mobbed deep in the Philadelphia end, Gretzky fell to the ice surrounded by teammates with expressions of disbelief writ large on their faces. This was a moment to remember, for no player will ever get to fifty goals faster.

WHY IT WON'T BE EQUALLED Gretzky himself has said this will be one of the most difficult records to break. To go on a hot streak during the season is common, but to keep it up for half a season requires another level of greatness altogether. A player needs a combination of consistency, good health, incredible teammates, and a coach willing to play him almost half a game, every game, and a rare combination of skill and perspicacity. As well, scoring is now so well below what it was in Gretzky's time that just scoring fifty goals in an eighty-two-game season is an incredible achievement. Only one player hit fifty in 2010–11 (Anaheim's Corey Perry), and in the last five years only ten players have hit fifty, the same number as reached fifty in 1981–82 alone.

GRETZKY (LEFT) PLAYFULLY WIPES THE CHEEK OF HIS
GOAL CHAMPION PREDECESSOR, PHIL ESPOSITO.

CHASING 100 Immediately after getting fifty in thirty-nine, the hockey world turned its attention to something it never considered remotely possible—100 goals in a single NHL season. Gretzky was halfway there and he still had more than half a season to go. "I think I can double everything," he said. "As long as the rest of the guys on the team keep playing the way they are, I think I'm capable of doubling what I've done so far."

Could he maintain this ridiculously torrid pace for an entire, eighty-game season? Yes, and no. Gretzky had five three-or-more goal games in the thirty-nine games of the streak, and he had another five after, but a two-week drought in March ended his hopes of reaching 100. Before the Montreal game on March 2, he had eighty-two goals in just sixty-six games. Getting eighteen goals in the last fourteen games hardly seemed impossible anymore. But between March 2–13, he didn't score once, a span of six games. In the end, he had ninety-two goals in eighty games, another record that seems untouchable.

GRETZKY WINS ART ROSS ON ASSISTS ALONE

THE RECORD On three occasions, Wayne Gretzky won the Art Ross Trophy by recording more assists than the next highest scorer had total points. For five years in a row, he won the Art Ross Trophy by a margin of at least seventy points over the second-place scorer.

HOW IT WAS DONE It all started in 1982–83. Wayne Gretzky led the league in scoring with seventy-one goals, 125 assists, 196 points. Second overall was Peter Stastny of Quebec, who had forty-seven goals, seventy-seven assists, and 124 points. The numbers are clear. Gretzky could have gone the entire season without scoring a single goal and still would have won the scoring title. Two years later, his assists total of 135 was the same as Jari Kurri's point total.

The next year, Gretzky blew the competition away, recording 163 assists and 215 points. Second in scoring was Mario Lemieux with 141 points. Gretzky could have not scored a goal (again) and still won the Art Ross by twenty-two points, a huge margin of victory any other year, any other player. Again the next year, 1986–87, Gretzky had 121 assists (and 183 total points) while teammate Jari Kurri was second in scoring with 108 points. Gretzky won the Art Ross Trophy a record ten times.

During his best years, Gretzky won the scoring title by margins of seventy-one points (in 1982–83), seventy-nine points, seventy-three points, seventy-four points, and seventy-five points. No one before or since ever came close to such margins. Mario Lemieux won by thirty-one points in 1988–89, and Phil Esposito twice won by twenty-six points (in 1971–72 and 1972–73). Gretzky made what was usually one of the more interesting races of the season's end into a one-man show, so lop-sided that he could have stopped playing at Christmas and still won the scoring title.

WHY IT WON'T BE EQUALLED

There is no metaphor or comparison to explain just how spectacular these three seasons are. No other player comes remotely close to having as many assists as any other player has points in the league. In fact, it isn't written down easily and isn't as glamourous sounding as "fifty in thirty-nine" or "215 points," but this achievement might well be the most untouchable of Gretzky's season records. No one scores that much; no one is so dominant. No one will do this again.

UNBEATABLE SEASON RECORDS

OTHER RECORD SEASONS Perhaps the only way to understand this record is to see what other great players before and since have done. Going back to 1940–41, Bill Cowley led all scorers with seventeen goals, forty-five assists, and sixty-two points. The second leading scorer was Bryan Hextall, with forty-four points. Still, his margin of victory would have been one point (between Cowley's assists and Hextall's total points), well behind Gretzky's record of twenty-two. This was the only other time a player had more assists than anyone else points, but in a forty-eight-game season and only sixty-two total points, this pales beside Gretzky's feat.

In 1970–71, Phil Esposito shattered all records with seventy-six goals, seventy-six assists, and 152 points. But Bobby Orr was right behind with 139, way ahead of Espo's assist total. The previous season, Orr was in the same vicinity as Gretzky, winning the scoring title with 120 points. His eighty-seven assists weren't too far behind Phil Esposito's point total of ninety-nine. This differential of twelve is as close as anyone got, with Cowley's exception.

ON FEBRUARY 24, 1982, GRETZKY SCORED
HIS SEVENTY-SEVENTH GOAL OF THE SEASON,
ECLIPSING PHIL ESPOSITO'S RECORD.

MICHAEL JORDAN

The only other player to lead his league in scoring ten times, Michael Jordan was to the NBA what Gretzky was to hockey. But Jordan's widest margin of victory came in 1986–87, the first time he led all NBA players in scoring. That year he had 3,041 points for the Chicago Bulls while runner-up Alex English had 2,345 with the Denver Nuggets. Jordan had 29.7 per cent more points than the number two player. But consider Gretzky's best year, 1983–84, when he won the scoring title with 205 points. Teammate Paul Coffey was second with 126. Gretzky had 63 per cent more points than the next best player in the league.

ALL-TIME POINTS AND ASSISTS So many records, it's tough to make sense of them all. Although Gretzky's single-season records of more assists than anyone else had points is sensational enough, the grand-daddy of them all has to be his career totals. Before he came into the league, it seemed unfathomable that someone could score more than Gordie Howe's 801 goals and 1,850 points. After all, it took him twenty-six years to reach that mark, and how often does a player come along who can have such longevity and production both?

By the time he retired, Gretzky had annihilated Howe's records to such a degree that, yes, he actually had more career assists than any other player in league history had points. In other words, forget about Gretzky's 894 goals being the all-time record. If he had zero goals, his 1,963 career assists would still put him ahead of Howe and Mark Messier, who is second overall with 1,887 points. As well, Gretzky averaged nearly two points a game for twenty years, a rate of production that only Mario Lemieux approached. (Gretzky averaged 1.92 points a game and Mario 1.88.)

GRETZKY'S FIFTY-ONE-GAME POINT-SCORING STREAK

THE RECORD From the start of the 1983–84 season on October 5, 1983, through to January 27, 1984, Wayne Gretzky recorded a point in fifty-one straight games.

HOW IT WAS DONE Wayne Gretzky was at the height of his powers when the 1983–84 season began. The Oilers had made it to the Stanley Cup Final before losing to the New York Islanders the previous season, and now knew what it would take to succeed. They were prepared to make whatever sacrifices were necessary to win. The twenty-two year old Gretzky was coming off another record-setting season in which he recorded 196 points, but he knew he could do more.

He started the year as if it were mid-season, getting a goal and assist on opening night against his favourite opponent, the Leafs, and carrying on with three-point nights against Winnipeg and Minnesota. On October 12, against Detroit, he had five points, and he followed that great night with games of two, three, and two points. Just seven games into the season, he already had twenty points. Gretzky kept scoring and scoring, leading the Oilers to one win after another. He had another five-point night against Washington, and four nights later, he had seven points against

Winnipeg. On November 19, against New Jersey, he had three goals and five assists in a 13–4 win over the hapless Devils, and he kept on going and going.

Soon enough, he had a point streak approaching his record of thirty games, and Las Vegas started to take bets that he'd get a point in every game that season. He flew past thirty games and kept adding to the totals. Gretzky had a close call in game forty-four, on January 11, 1984, when his only point came via an empty-net goal with just two seconds left in the game, a 3-1 win over Chicago. Finally, on January 28, the Oilers lost at home to Los Angeles, 4–2, and Gretzky was held off the scoresheet. And just as he had good luck to keep the streak going, he had bad luck to end it. He made a great pass to Charlie Huddy for an open-net goal on a two-on-one in the first period, but Huddy shot wide. "I jokingly told Charlie after the period that that one might be my last chance," Gretzky confessed.

In those fifty-one games, Gretzky had 153 points, averaging exactly three a game. Going back further, Gretzky had a point in his previous nine

OTHER TOP NHL STREAKS

Gretzky established an impressive point-scoring streak in 1982–83, when he went thirty games with at least one point. In addition to his fifty-one-game streak, he had another of thirty-nine games in 1985–86, the third-longest of all time. The second longest belongs to Mario Lemieux, who had a point in forty-six consecutive games with Pittsburgh in 1989–90. As with so much of his career, though, the streak ended not because of a bad game, but because of injury, sustained the night of February 14, 1990, at Madison Square Garden. His back had been causing him pain for weeks, but he played on. On this night he went to the dressing room for the second intermission and simply couldn't continue. A streak that started Halloween night 1989 ended Valentine's Day, 1990.

JOE DIMAGGIO CONNECTED FOR A BASE HIT UP THE MIDDLE IN CLEVELAND
ON JULY 16, 1941, STRETCHING HIS STREAK TO 56 GAMES.

DIMAGGIO'S 56-GAME HITTING STREAK—EASIER OR TOUGHER? The closest comparison to Gretzky's scoring streak is Joe DiMaggio's record of hitting safely in fifty-six baseball games in 1941. Of course, the numbers fifty-six and fifty-one suggest something close, but hockey fans are likely to argue Gretzky's is the more difficult record and baseball fans DiMaggio's. The most telling difference is surely the era. Seventy years ago, the only media were newspapers and radio, so the daily pressures of continuing a successful run were nowhere near what they were for Gretzky in the early 1980s. But whether it is more difficult to get a base hit or a goal or assist is to compare apples to oranges. Is it easier to beat a goalie with a shot or get a hit off a pitcher?

Surely getting a hit is much easier. After all, the all-time record for hits by a player is held by Pete Rose with 4,256, way more points than Gretzky, Gordie Howe, Mark Messier, or Marcel Dionne. As well, a baseball game routinely has twenty hits between the two teams, but much less frequently are the times a hockey game will have twenty total points between the teams (goals and assists). Scoring is also much higher in baseball than hockey, so offence, as measured by the numbers in each sport, is much greater in baseball. In truth, Gretzky's fifty-one-game streak is far more unreachable than DiMaggio's fifty-six-game streak, but it's probably nitpicking to argue as much. Neither record will be equaled.

games to end the 1982–83 season, but the NHL does not carry over its records. Key to ending the streak was a strategy used by the Kings' interim head coach Rogie Vachon. He put out his best defencemen, Jay Wells and Mark Hardy, every time Gretzky stepped on the ice.

WHY IT WON'T BE EQUALLED Great scorers are great because they are consistent, but being consistent is an ever more psychological phenomenon. Even if a player were to start a streak that extended thirty games or more, the pressure from fans and media, the constant barrage of questions about the streak would almost be enough of a negative force on its own to scuttle it. Even in 2010–11, when Sidney Crosby had a streak that reached twenty-five games, the scrutiny of the already most-scrutinized player was tremendous—and he was only halfway to Gretzky's mark! If a series of fifty-one opponents wouldn't prevent a player from reaching Gretzky's record, the external pressures would.

Gretzky also suffered a shoulder injury during that Los Angeles game in which he didn't get a point, and he ended up missing the next six games. He returned as though no time had passed, however, scoring twice and adding two assists in a 7–3 win against Winnipeg. In fact, he was held pointless in only two games of the final twenty-two of the season, meaning that overall his record on the year was seventy-four games played, points in seventy-one, and six games missed because of injury. He finished with eighty-seven goals and 205 points, and in the playoffs the Oilers went all the way, winning their first Stanley Cup. In 1984–85, he played all eighty games and had points in seventy-five, and the year after he again played eighty games and had points in an extraordinary seventy-seven of those games, totaling 215 points, his finest season ever.

TWO YEARS IN ONE—GRETZKY GETS 215 POINTS

THE RECORD Wayne Gretzky played all eighty games of the 1985–86 season, setting a record with 215 points (52 goals, 163 assists).

HOW IT WAS DONE By the time the 1985–86 season had arrived the only thing that surprised anyone about Gretzky anymore was that he continued to surprise, playing at such a high level that no one could match him. When Martina Navratilova was the number one women's player in tennis—by a wide margin—John McEnroe famously said she was trying to become number zero. Gretzky was zero in the NHL, such was his dominance.

In 1981–82, he became the first player to eclipse 200 points, finishing with 212, and in 1983–84 and 1984–85 he passed 200 again. But in 1985–86, he set a record that will never be equaled, scoring 215 points in eighty games. Although he never approached his record fifty-one-game point-scoring streak, he failed to get a point in a game only three times all season. Of the seventy-seven games in which he did get a point, he had sixteen games with one point, twenty-one games with two points, nineteen games with three points, twelve games with four points, four games with five points, three games with six points, and two games with seven points.

What was most aston- ishing was his ability to make a mid-career tran- sition from a scorer who could pass to a passer who could score. Con- sider that in his first season he had fifty-one goals, a number that in- creased to fifty-five the year after. Then came the four most explosive and game-changing sea- sons for him. Gretzky went from fifty-five to ninety-two, then seventy-one, eighty-seven, and seventy-three goals. Only twice more in his career did he reach fifty (fifty-two in 1985–86 and sixty-two the next year). Meanwhile, though, he was increasing his assists totals and set- ting records in that column that defied logic. Only thirteen times has a player reached 100 assists in a year, and Gretzky is responsible for eleven of that number.

His record 215-point season was a result of a record for assists in a season (163) more than it was a combination of goals and assists. Not surprisingly, linemate Jari Kurri led the league with sixty-eight goals while defenceman Paul Coffey set a record by getting forty-eight goals. The Oilers scored 426 goals this season (the second-highest total ever behind their 446 in 1983–84), and Gretzky was involved in more than half.

ONLY 200-POINT SEASONS

Almost as if Fate were taunting Mario Lemieux, the great number 66 has come close to Gretzky in several records, but for one reason or another— usually health—he has fallen just short. The 200-point season is another case in point. Gretzky had 200 points or more in a season four times, the only player ever to hit 200. But in 1988–89, Mario had 199 in seventy-six games. He missed four games because of injuries, but surely had he played even one more game he would have reached 200. Instead, one point short, Gretzky alone can lay claim to the double-century milestone.

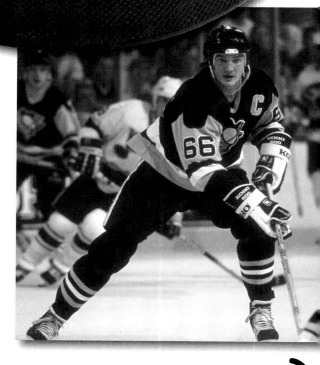

GRETZKY SOMETIMES A SCORER, SOMETIMES PASSER, ALWAYS OFFENSIVE

The dual nature of Gretzky's offence is unique in the game's history. A star scorer such as Maurice Richard, for instance, always had more goals than assists in any given season. A pure passer such as Joe Thornton always had many more assists than goals. Gretzky somehow was both a scorer and passer at the same time. Of course, he holds the record for the most goals in a season with ninety-two, and four times he had more than seventy goals. He's a scorer, right? Well, at the other end, he won the Art Ross Trophy three times without even getting forty-two goals! And, he led the league in assists for the first thirteen seasons of his career, a spectacular level of consistency and production via passing alone.

WHY IT WON'T BE EQUALLED To be clear—Gretzky actually had four times more multi-point games than he had games with a single point. This defies all logic, all odds. Players always have fewer multi-point games than single-point games because, of course, it's that much more difficult to get two or three points in a game than it is to get one. Not so for Gretzky. In the post-Gretzky era, sanity has again ruled, and any player who gets 100 points in a season is considered a superstar. Since Gretzky retired in 1999, the top scorer in any one season was Joe Thornton, who had 125 points for Boston/San Jose in 2005–06.

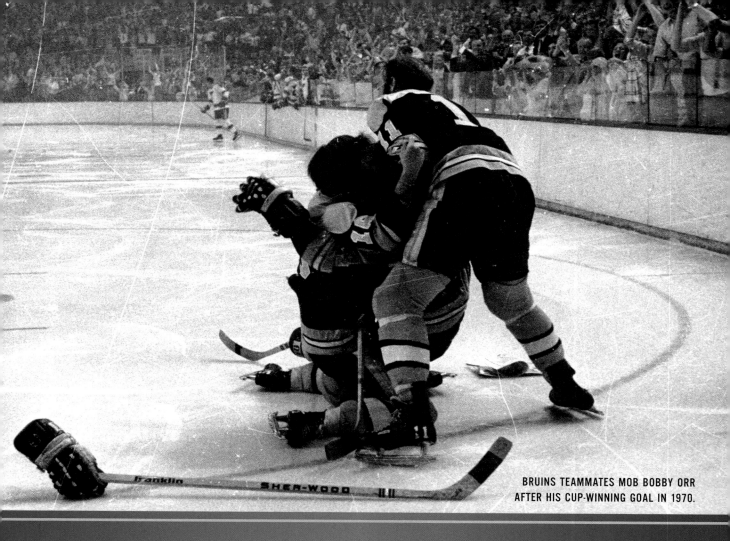

BRUINS TEAMMATES MOB BOBBY ORR
AFTER HIS CUP-WINNING GOAL IN 1970.

ASSISTS AND GOALS RECORDS IN A SEASON Bobby Orr set the standard for assists when he got 102 in the 1970–71 season. The only other time anyone has recorded more than 100 came during the high-scoring period of 1980 to 1991. During that time, 100 assists or more were recorded twelve times. Gretzky did it eleven of those times and Mario Lemieux once, in 1988–89. In a similar period of time, 1981–93, there were thirteen seasons of more than seventy goals. Gretzky accounted for four of those. Brett Hull had eighty-six goals in 1990–91, second all-time to Gretzky's ninety-two, while Mario Lemieux had two seasons of seventy or more. Jari Kurri was the first European to reach that mark when he got seventy-one in 1984–85, playing alongside Gretzky. Teemu Selanne hit seventy-six as a rookie in 1992–93 with the Winnipeg Jets, another record that won't be equaled.

COFFEY PASSES ORR WITH FORTY-EIGHT GOALS IN A SEASON

THE RECORD In 1985–86, defenceman Paul Coffey of the Edmonton Oilers scored forty-eight goals in an eighty-game season, two better than the previous record holder, Bobby Orr.

HOW IT WAS DONE Coffey played seventy-nine of the Oilers' eighty games in 1985–86, but his season didn't start like a record-breaking one. In the first game, a 4–3 win over Winnipeg, Coffey didn't record a point—but he did get into a fight. He got a pair of assists in his next game, but it wasn't until game three that he counted his first goal (first two, in fact). Two games later, he had another two-goal effort. Coffey then went twenty-seven games before he had another multi-goal game, but that night—December 20, 1985—was a sensational one. He had a hat trick, two assists, and a fight, recording a Gordie Howe hat trick (goal, assist, fight) and a five-point night in a 9–4 win over Los Angeles. Two nights later, he had five assists in a 7–5 loss to the Jets.

It wasn't until January that Coffey really started to score. He had ten goals that month and followed with eleven in February. That pre-Christmas hat trick was his only one of the season, but three times he managed a Gordie Howe hat trick, a remarkable record for any player, let alone a defenceman.

Still, Coffey also managed twelve two-goal games, and on March 14, he tied a league record with a pair of goals, six assists, and eight points.

Bobby Orr had forty-six goals in 1974–75, also an eighty-game season, and Coffey approached that record as his 1985–86

THIRTY IS RARE

In the long history of the NHL, only eight defencemen have scored thirty goals or more in a season. Orr did it five times, Coffey four, and Denis Potvin three. All others did it only once—Doug Wilson (1981–82, Chicago), Kevin Hatcher (1992–93, Washington), Ray Bourque (1983–84, Boston), Phil Housley (1983–84, Buffalo), and Mike Green (2008–09, Washington). Coffey also scored forty in 1983–84, making him the only blue-liner to have two, forty-goal seasons. Orr had thirty-three goals in 1969–70, the first defenceman to crack thirty, and all thirty-plus seasons, excepting Green's, occurred in the twenty-four years after Orr's initial record.

WASHINGTON'S MIKE GREEN.

SOMETIMES, IT'S NOT THE STATS Coffey played for Canada at the Canada Cup in 1981, 1984, 1987, and 1991, as well as the 1996 World Cup of Hockey. He was victorious three times and runner-up the other two, but there was one defensive play at the 1984 Canada Cup for which he is as well remembered as any rush he ever made. In overtime of the semi-finals against the Soviet Union, he found himself the lone man back on a two-on-one against Vladimir Kovin and Mikhail Varnakov. An odd-man rush for the Soviets of this era was pretty much a certain goal, but Coffey broke up the rush expertly, got control of the puck, and moved it up ice to John Tonelli in one fluid motion. Coffey then got a return pass at the point in the Soviets' end. His shot was deflected in front by Mike Bossy in the slot, and Canada won the game, 3–2. The team then went on to beat Sweden in the finals.

MIKE BOSSY CELEBRATES VICTORY IN THE 1984, SCORING THE WINNING GOAL DESPITE BEING CLOSELY GUARDED BY SOVIET DEFENCEMAN VLADIMIR KOVIN.

season was winding down. He tied and broke the record on April 2 in an 8–4 home win against Vancouver, and two nights later he added to his total with a final goal against Calgary. Coffey was held without a point in the team's last game, ending with forty-eight goals, a record for scoring by a defenceman that won't be equaled.

WHY IT WON'T BE EQUALLED The era of the rushing defenceman is dead, and teams play such incredibly effective defence that no defenceman can join the rush or create offence to the extent that Orr and Coffey used to. Add to the fact that Coffey was perhaps the best skater the game has ever known, and that he played on a team that scored more goals than any other in NHL history, and you get a recipe for success that has no chance of being equaled.

"FINNISH FLASH" SCORES SEVENTY-SIX GOALS AS A ROOKIE

THE RECORD Winnipeg Jets rookie right winger Teemu Selanne scored seventy-six goals and 132 total points in his first NHL season, 1992–93.

HOW IT WAS DONE Teemu Selanne made his NHL debut on October 6, 1992, a 4–1 home win against Detroit. The twenty-two-year-old had been drafted tenth overall by the Jets four years earlier, but played in the top Finnish league for three more years with Jokerit, as well as competing in the 1992 Olympics, before coming to the NHL.

In this respect, he wasn't a pure rookie, but his three pro seasons of top-level hockey in Finland and international experience didn't count against him when he joined the NHL. He had two assists in his first game, October 6, 1992, and scored his first goal two nights later, in game number two.

Selanne was nothing if not sensational. He had speed to burn, a great shot, and tremendous confidence. He scored in his third game and had a hat trick in his fifth. Then, after a goalless game, he scored in five straight to reach eleven goals in his first ten NHL games. He had a slump that lasted four games, but over the course of the season he was both prolific and consistent. That four-game slump was the longest of his season. He had one four-goal game (February 28, in a 7–6 win over Minnesota), four hat tricks, and twelve two-goal games in the eighty-four game season.

He was held without a point only seventeen times all year and finished the season with points in his final thirteen games, his longest streak of the season. It was during his four-goal game that he hit fifty on the season, a plateau reached by a rookie only four times in the history of the NHL (Mike Bossy

FIFTY-GOAL ROOKIES

If scoring 100 points for a first-year player is rare, scoring fifty goals is rarer. Only four names grace this list, starting at the top, of course, with Selanne, whose seventy-six goals are untouchable for a rookie. Mike Bossy, a pure scorer with a wickedly quick release, had fifty-three goals in 1977–78 (91 total points) and Alexander Ovechkin had fifty-two in his first year. The only name that's not on the 100-point list is Joe Nieuwendyk who scored fifty-one goals for Calgary in 1987–88. He finished with ninety-two points.

100-POINT ROOKIES

Only seven times has a first-year player reached the 100-point mark. The first to do it was Peter Stastny, in 1980–81, but his achievement needs an asterisk because by the time Stastny was able to defect from Czechoslovakia to play in the NHL, he was twenty-four years old and a veteran of five years of pro hockey with Slovan Bratislava. For the same reason, further controversy ensued when he won the Calder Trophy. Many felt he wasn't a true rookie. The next year, Dale Hawerchuk, a true eighteen-year-old straight out of junior, reached 103 points and also won the Calder. Three years later, nineteen-year-old, Mario Lemieux made it exactly to 100 by scoring his forty-third goal on the final day of the season, a 7–3 loss at Washington.

Joining Selanne in 1992–93 was Joe Juneau, a twenty-five-year-old who had played fourteen games the previous year after attending RPI for four years. Selanne won the Calder Trophy, but there was also concern for his case as well because he had played top level hockey for Jokerit for the previous three years. Ditto for Ovechkin, who had played in the Russian league for four years with Dynamo Moscow. Sidney Crosby, eighteen when he hit 100, was a rookie by anyone's definition.

DALE HAWERCHUK OF THE WINNIPEG JETS.

in 1977–78; Joe Nieuwendyk, 1987–88; and, Alexander Ovechkin, 2005–06). Bossy's record of fifty-three came tumbling down in Selanne's next game, his sixty-third of the season, a hat trick effort against Quebec on March 2, still with sixteen games left in the season. After that, every goal Selanne scored improved his own mark, until he got number seventy-six in his final game. He added an assist in that game to give him 132 points, another record that will stand the test of time.

The previous first-year points record belonged to Peter Stastny—another player deemed a rookie despite a long career in Europe—who had 109 points in 1980–81. Selanne tied and beat that mark in his seventy-fourth game when he had two goals and an assist on March 23 against the Maple Leafs.

WHY IT WON'T BE EQUALLED The days of 132-point years from seasoned veterans are over, and the NHL is so fast and young nowadays that rookies are happy simply to make the roster for their first season. A great rookie is someone who plays responsibly in his own end and contributes to the offence, not someone who leads his team in scoring. If Alexander Ovechkin (52 goals, 106 points) and Sidney Crosby (39 goals, 102 points) can't come close to Selanne's record, no one can—at least, not for a very long time.

DEFINING A ROOKIE

The NHL has specific and detailed rules about what constitutes a rookie. A player must first of all be under twenty-six years of age as of September 15 of his first season. As well, he can't have played more than twenty-five games of any previous NHL season or six or more games in any two previous seasons in any major professional league. Because the NHL considers its league to be the best in the world, "major professional league" refers generally only to the NHL, which is why Selanne or Ovechkin or any European is eligible for the Calder Trophy so long as he's under twenty-six years of age.

NOT JUST ANOTHER KID, SID THE YOUNGEST TO 100 POINTS

THE RECORD On April 17, 2006, the second-last day of the 2005–06 season, Pittsburgh's Sidney Crosby recorded three assists to become the youngest player to reach 100 points in a season. He was eighteen years, 253 days old.

HOW IT WAS DONE Sidney Crosby's timing was perfect. The star had played two years for Rimouski in the QMJHL, from 2003 to 2005, and during the second of those years he garnered more attention than might normally be expected because the NHL lockout cancelled the pro season, leaving fans with little other than amateur and international hockey to watch. In the summer of 2005, the Penguins won the right to draft first overall after a lottery determined the order, and, right on schedule, Crosby made his pro debut with Pittsburgh on October 5, 2005, a 5–1 road loss to New Jersey.

Crosby assisted on the only Pittsburgh goal early in the third period. He was only eighteen years, fifty-nine days old. Crosby had points in each of his first six games. He had his first multi-point game in his third game, getting a goal and two assists in a 7–6 OT loss to Boston in the Pens' home opener. He had his first multi-goal game on November 3, against the

Islanders. In all, he had points in sixty of the team's eighty-two games, had twenty-eight multi-point games, and had multi-goal games six times (although he didn't record a hat trick all season). He was neck-and-neck with Alexander Ovechkin for the rookie scoring lead, the two mega-stars miles ahead of all others.

The biggest difference between the two was that Ovechkin was two years older than Crosby and had played pro hockey in Russia for the previous four years. On the second-last day of the season, though, Sid the Kid, as he was called then, got his ninety-eighth, ninety-ninth, and 100th points of the season, in a 6–1 home win over the Islanders. He became only the second eighteen-year-old to reach the century mark after Dale Hawerchuk, who reached 103 points in the 1981–82 season.

COMPARING TO GRETZKY Gretzky was born in January and started his pro career at age seventeen in the WHA. As a result, he was half a year older than Crosby when he made his NHL debut with the Edmonton Oilers in the fall of 1979. Nevertheless, Gretzky reached 100 points in his sixty-second game, several weeks after his nineteenth birthday, but he went on to ever greater scoring exploits which Crosby, in this more defence-first era, hasn't been able to match (no one has). Gretzky didn't become captain until he was twenty-two and he didn't win his first Stanley Cup until he was twenty-three.

But one thing Gretzky did that was something no one else will ever do was to lead the U20 championship in scoring at age sixteen. At a time when any kid is just happy to be playing U20, Gretzky dominated the 1978 event and announced his greatness on the international stage in the process. However, one thing Crosby did at age twenty-two that Gretzky never did was win Olympic gold and score the golden goal to win that gold. For that Crosby has already earned his place in the game's history.

The start of Crosby's career was a veritable litany of "the youngest" records. He was also the youngest player to be voted a starter at the All-Star Game, youngest named to the First All-Star Team, youngest to be named team captain, and youngest captain to win the Stanley Cup. At the 2004 World U20 (Junior) Championship, the sixteen-year-old was also the youngest player to score a goal in tournament history. He also became the youngest player to win the Art Ross Trophy and Lester B. Pearson Award. At the 2006 World Championship, the eighteen-year-old became the youngest player to lead the tournament in scoring. And, beating even Wayne Gretzky, Crosby was also the youngest player to get to 200 career points, accomplishing the feat at age nineteen years, 207 days, on March 2, 2007, against Carolina.

CROSBY CUTS AROUND SLOVAKIA'S IVAN CIERNIK DURING THE 2006 WORLD CHAMPIONSHIP.

WHY IT WON'T BE EQUALLED Apart from tremendous skill, of course, a player needs luck to get near this record. To wit, a player becomes draft eligible if he turns eighteen by September 15 of his draft year. So, for instance, Crosby was born August 7, 1987, and would turn eighteen on that date in 2005. So, when he was actually drafted in July 2005, he was still only seventeen, but by the time he played his first NHL game he had turned eighteen. So, two things must happen for any player to beat Crosby. First, he must be born closer to September 15, to make him that few days or weeks younger come the start of the season. Then, he must hit 100 points earlier in the season.

Hawerchuk reached 100 in the team's seventy-fourth game and Crosby in Pittsburgh's eighty-first game. Now, let's look at Wayne Gretzky's 1983–84 season. He was twenty-two at the time and in the prime of his career, and he got his 100th point in the team's thirty-fourth game, on December 18, 1983. So, if every element were perfectly lined up, a player could be born on September 14 of a given year and score his 100th point on December 18 or so, if he were (a) lucky with birthdate and (b) as skilled at eighteen as Gretzky was at twenty-two. The youngest possible date a player might get his 100th point, then, would be about eighteen years and three months. Crosby was about eighteen years and eight months. Considering only two eighteen-year-olds have ever hit 100, it's safe to say the chances of this ideal circumstance happening is less than winning the lottery.

PHIL ESPOSITO NOTCHES HIS 100TH POINT OF THE 1968–69 SEASON AGAINST JOE DALEY, THE FIRST PLAYER TO REACH THE PLATEAU.

FIRST TO 100 The 100-point mark was for a long time a coveted and never-attained pinnacle in the NHL. While Maurice Richard had fifty goals in fifty games in 1944–45, no player got particularly close to 100 points until the 1960s. Gordie Howe had ninety-five in 1952–53, and Dickie Moore of Montreal had ninety-six in 1958–59. Teammate Bernie Geoffrion had ninety-five again in 1960–61, the same year he became the second player after Richard to score fifty in a season (although "Boom Boom" did it in sixty-four games). Bobby Hull and Stan Mikita, both of Chicago, got a little closer in consecutive years, 1965–66 and 1966–67, when they had ninety-seven points each year.

But in 1968–69, Phil Esposito blew the roof off the mark, scoring his 100th point in the team's sixty-second game in the seventy-six-game season and finishing with 126. Of course, the schedule played a large role in his achievement. Previously, Howe, Hull, Mikita, Geoffrion, et al had played in a seventy-game season, and these extra games helped add to Espo's totals. But even still, he got his 100th point in game number sixty-two, which helped legitimize the record vis-a-vis his predecessors.

SIDNEY CROSBY IS CONGRATULATED BY TEAM CAPTAIN AND OWNER
MARIO LEMIEUX AFTER SCORING A GOAL.

UNBEATABLE
GAME
RECORDS

JOE MALONE'S SCORING SPREE

THE RECORD On January 31, 1920, Joe Malone of the Quebec Bulldogs scored seven goals in a single game against the Toronto St. Patricks.

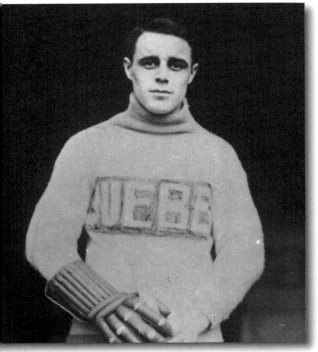

QUEBEC

HOW IT WAS DONE It was the twelfth game of the 1919–20 season for the Bulldogs. The season had begun on Christmas Day, 1919, and Quebec won only one of its first eleven games. It was also the last game of the season's first half. In the NHL's early days, the season was divided into two distinct parts, the first-place team of the first half playing the first-place team of the second half for the league title at season's end.

But on this night, before just 1,200 spectators, Joe Malone went wild, setting a goal-scoring record that has not been beat in the ninety-two years since.

Malone opened the scoring early in the first period by claiming the puck at centre and skating through the entire Toronto team before beating Ivan "Mike" Mitchell for the game's first goal. This was Malone's only goal of the period, and after twenty minutes the Bulldogs led the St. Pats by a 3–2 score.

Malone began the second period in style, converting a great pass from Harry Mummery just fifty-five seconds in to make it a 4–2 game. It was his first of three goals in the period. The two players teamed up again midway through the period after Cy Denneny had brought the St. Pats to within one. Again, Mummery made the pass and Malone "shot the goal," as they used to say. Malone got his fourth of the game near the end of the period, and the Bulldogs now led 6–4.

In the final period, Toronto put Howie Lockhart in goal in place of Mitchell, but that changed little. The St. Pats got two goals early sandwiched around a George Carey goal to make it 7–6 Quebec, but in the last half of the period it was all Malone. He scored the final three goals, his fifth, sixth, and seventh of the night.

The *Quebec Chronicle* wrote that, "Joe Malone was the bright star. The lanky forward had his biggest night of the year, setting up an individual performance that has not yet been equaled this year." The suggestion was that it was very much a scoring outburst that could be achieved again. Nine decades later, we're still waiting. No player since has scored as much in one NHL game.

WHY IT WON'T BE EQUALLED In the ninety-four-year history of the NHL, a player has scored six goals in a game only seven times. More

SCORING ERA

Malone was not alone as a scoring star in this period of the NHL. Indeed, this 1919–20 season saw four other players average a goal a game. Right behind him was Montreal's Newsy Lalonde who had thirty-seven goals in twenty-three games. Frank Nighbor of Ottawa had twenty-six goals in twenty-three games, and Toronto's Corb Denneny and Reg Noble each had twenty-four goals in the same number of games for the St. Pats.

GOAL A GAMERS Averaging a goal a game was easier in a four-team league with only twenty-four games on the schedule, but much tougher in a lengthier season with thirty teams. Maurice Richard set the standard in 1944–45, scoring fifty in fifty, but it wasn't until 1981–82 that Wayne Gretzky became the first modern star to average more than a goal a game. His ninety-two goals in eighty games is still a record, but few remember his 1983–84 season which was even more productive. That year he had eighty-seven goals in just seventy-four games, an average of 1.18 per game, slightly better than 1981–82 (1.15). Mario Lemieux had eighty-five goals in seventy-six games in 1988–89 (1.12 per game), and Brett Hull had eighty-six goals in seventy-eight games (1.10), the only players to score an average of at least once a game over the course of a full season.

WAYNE GRETZKY CELEBRATES ONE
OF HIS 894 CAREER GOALS.

telling, five of those came before the end of the Second World War. Since then, Red Berenson scored six for St. Louis, on November 7, 1968, in an 8–0 win over Philadelphia in the Spectrum. More famously, Darryl Sittler scored six times during his ten-point night of February 7, 1976, an 11–4 home win over Don Cherry's Boston Bruins. In the thirty-five years since, no one has scored more than five in a game, and given the defensive nature of the modern game, it's impossible to conceive of someone scoring seven. If Gretzky, Lemieux, Crosby, Ovechkin, Yzerman, and dozens of other of the greatest players ever can't do it, who can?

JOE MALONE.

WHO IS JOE MALONE?

Malone was a star for the National Hockey Association's (predecessor of the NHL) Bulldogs from 1910–17. He was nicknamed "Phantom" for his ability to avoid checks and for his stickhandling wizardry. Although the era was different and the numbers skewed by rule differences, Malone set a record by scoring forty-four goals in just twenty games with the Montreal Canadiens in 1917–18, the first NHL season. In all, he had 143 goals in 126 career NHL games before retiring in 1924. Most impressive about his seven goals, however, is that the feat came with a terrible team. The Bulldogs had a record of 4–20 in 1919–20 and scored only ninety-one goals. His thirty-nine on the season means he alone accounted for 43 per cent of his team's offence that year.

RED WINGS AND MAROONS PLAY THREE GAMES IN ONE NIGHT

THE RECORD In game one of the best-of-five semi-finals of the 1936 playoffs, March 24, the Detroit Red Wings defeated the Montreal Maroons by a 1–0 score in a game that was decided by a Mud Bruneteau goal at 16:30 of the sixth overtime period. Played in Montreal, it remains the longest overtime game ever.

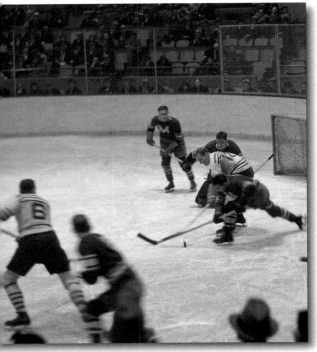

THE MONTREAL MAROONS IN GAME ACTION AGAINST THE TORONTO MAPLE LEAFS DURING THE 1930S.

HOW IT WAS DONE The Maroons and the Red Wings finished first in their divisions and met in the first round of the playoffs. The opening game of the series started on March 24, and ended in the wee hours of March 25, some six hours by the clock after the opening faceoff. Normie Smith got the shut-out, and Mud Bruneteau scored the winner. The next night they played again, in Montreal. Smith shut out the Maroons once again, and the team then finished the sweep with a 2–1 win in Detroit three nights later. The Wings then went on to defeat the Maple Leafs 3–1 in a best-of-five Final to win its first Stanley Cup.

Bruneteau was an unlikely hero, having only recently been recalled from the Detroit Olympics, but it was, in many respects, Smith who was the best player in the game. Time and again he stopped sure goals from the Maroons to extend the game. In all, he stopped ninety shots while Lorne Chabot faced sixty-eight in the Maroons goal.

GOALIE LORNE CHABOT.

The winning goal came off a nice pass from Hec Kilrea, and Bruneteau's shot beat Lorne Chabot cleanly at exactly 2:25 am local time. It had started at 8:30 pm the previous evening. The game pushed the players to the very edge of their physical capacity. Doc Holst, writing the game review in the *Detroit Free Press*, described one play: "Both teams started the sixth period just pretending they had energy. Once, Wentworth took a weak swing on a loose puck and fell on the ice."

GOALIE JOHN SORENSEN CELEBRATES
BREAKING THE WORLD RECORD FOR
THE LONGEST HOCKEY GAME, ON
FEBRUARY 21, 2011.

LONGEST GAME EVER—GUINNESS

The Guinness Book of World Records lists as the "longest marathon playing ice hockey" to be exactly 242 hours, set by Brent Saik and friends at Saiker's Acres in Strathcona, Alberta, February 11–21, 2011. The game was the brainchild of Dr. Brent Saik himself, and it was played to raise funds for the Cross Cancer Institute. Previous world records had been set by Saik in 2003, 2005, and 2008. The score was 2,067–2,005 with Jamie Dehr leading all goalscorers with 311!

In a remarkably classy move, Chabot later gave Bruneteau the game-winning puck, saying, "Here—I thought you might like to have this."

The best chance to end the game earlier came at the start of the fourth overtime when Hooley Smith of the Maroons was penalized for cross-checking, but the Red Wings could do little damage with the extra skater.

WHY IT WON'T BE EQUALLED The simple fact that this record has stood for seventy-five years is testament enough to its invincibility. The second-longest game occurred three years earlier, on April 3, 1993, when Toronto and Boston played early into a sixth overtime before the Leafs' Ken Doraty scored at 4:46 of that period. The next four longest games all belong to the modern era, yet none of them are particularly close to Bruneteau's record.

On May 4, 2000, Philadelphia and Pittsburgh played a marathon game that ended midway through a fifth OT period. Keith Primeau scored for the Flyers at 12:01 to end the game, but that is still almost a period and a half shy of the record. The only other game ever to go to a fifth period was played on April 24, 2003, when Anaheim and Dallas kept going until Petr Sykora scored just forty-eight seconds into the fifth period. And that's it. Thousands of playoff games, only four going to a fifth OT and only one going until the near the end of a sixth. Wings–Maroons, Bruneteau, and nearly three complete hockey games in one night. It's a record unlikely ever to be beat.

LONGEST GAME EVER—COMPETITIVE

The longest game ever played under the auspices of Hockey Canada occurred on March 2, 2011, during a women's game of the OUA finals. Queen's Gaels defeated the Guelph Gryphons by a 2–1 score when Morgan McHaffie scored at 17:14 of the sixth overtime. Playing time was ten minutes less than the 1936 NHL game, though, because the first OT was ten minutes and only subsequent overtimes were standard twenty minutes. It was game one of a best-of-three series. It started at 7:37 pm on March 2 and ended at 12:52 am on March 3. The game went to overtime when Queen's Becky Conroy tied the game at 19:55 of the third period.

OTHER LEAGUES, LONG GAMES Not only does the Detroit–Maroons game set a record for the NHL, no other league can claim a game as long. In the AHL, the longest game was played on April 24, 2008, between the Philadelphia Phantoms (the Flyers' farm team) and the Albany River Rats (farm team of the New Jersey Devils). That game was extended until 2:58 of the fifth overtime, when Ryan Potulny scored for the Phantoms. In ECHL play, the Elmira Jackals and Trenton Devils played 66:10 of overtime before the Jackals prevailed early in the fourth overtime. In NCAA play, the longest game was played between Quinnipiac University and Union College. Greg Holt scored the winner for Quinnipac at 10:12 of the fifth overtime.

BEP GUIDOLIN A CHILD IN THE NHL

THE RECORD On November 12, 1942, Bep Guidolin played his first NHL game for the Boston Bruins. He was sixteen years, 338 days old, the youngest player ever to appear in the league. The game, played at Maple Leaf Gardens, was won by the home side, 3–1.

HOW IT WAS DONE The war years were difficult ones for the NHL as it tried to keep operations running while losing dozens of players to military service. Boston was hit as hard as any team, but without the development system of Toronto or Montreal, it had to find any players of quality who could fill in. Guidolin, although young, was a rising star with the Oshawa Generals, having helped the team to the Memorial Cup in the spring of 1942. Just a few months later, he made the Bruins and played the season for them, scoring seven goals.

He made his debut at Maple Leaf Gardens in Boston's fourth game, wearing number 12, playing on a line with Don Gallinger and Bill Shill. Vice president and general manager Art Ross named the young threesome the Sprout Line. Guidolin's situation was strange, to be sure. The previous month, when the Bruins held their training camp in Montreal, Guidolin reported to the Bruins and even played an exhibition game for them against an army team in Cornwall. No

INTERNATIONAL YOUNGSTERS

While the rights of NHL players starts at draft time, international hockey is dictated by national federations and doesn't have the same restrictions. As a result, some very young players have made history in one way or another. For instance, Mark Howe, son of Gordie, played for the United States at the 1972 Olympics at age sixteen—and won a silver medal. Indeed, he was the youngest Olympian in men's hockey. Sandor Miklos of Hungary, however, was two months shy of his sixteenth birthday when he played at the 1931 World Championship.

sooner was that game over than he left the Bruins and returned to the Generals, but Ross asked the CAHA (Canadian Amateur Hockey Association, the governing body for amateur hockey in Canada, now called Hockey Canada) to suspend Guidolin because he had accepted a contract offer from the Bruins during camp.

The move was pure desperation on Ross's part. The Bruins had lost their first three games to start the season, and were last in the league with only three goals scored to twenty-one allowed. Guidolin scored his first goal on November 24, 1942, in a 5–5 tie with Chicago, becoming the youngest player to score in an NHL game as well (age 16 years, 350 days). Lost in the history-making night was the NHL debut of another youngster, Toronto's nineteen-year-old Jack McLean. He had a goal and two assists playing alongside Gaye Stewart and Bud Poile, the Kid Line dominating play all night.

WHY IT WON'T BE EQUALLED It is not within the realm of reason to believe the NHL will ever allow a sixteen-year-old to play in the league

GORDIE HOWE (CENTRE) CAME BACK TO HOCKEY TO PLAY WITH HIS SONS MARTY (LEFT) AND MARK.

YOUNGEST WOMEN

On the women's side, even younger players have appeared at the highest level. Hayley Wickenheiser made her debut at the 1994 World Women's Championship when she was only fifteen, and Swedish goalie Kim Martin was only thirty-six days past her fifteenth birthday when she played at the 2001 World Championship. She was just fifteen years, 350 days old when she made her Olympics debut a year later, in Salt Lake City. There have been no fewer than six girls who played at the World Championship while still only fourteen years old, the youngest being Iris Holzer of Switzerland who was, incredibly, only fifteen days past her fourteenth birthday when she appeared at the inaugural World Women's Championship in 1990 in Ottawa.

again. There are strict rules about the Entry Draft, and it's simply not a legal possibility for anyone under eighteen to appear in a game. Even if war were to break out and players headed off to service again, there are so many pro players in minor leagues and European leagues that NHL teams could easily flesh out their roster with players over eighteen.

HAYLEY WICKENHEISER WAS A TEEN SENSATION WHEN SHE JOINED TEAM CANADA.

HARRY LUMLEY WAS THE YOUNGEST GOALIE IN NHL HISTORY.

YOUNGEST GOALIE While Guidolin was the youngest skater ever to appear in the NHL, Harry Lumley was the youngest goalie. Of course, this also came about during the war. He was the property of the Detroit Red Wings during his rookie season of 1943–44, but he played for both the Red Wings and New York Rangers that year. In the case of the former, he appeared in two games, giving up thirteen goals and losing both. The first was a 6–2 loss to the Rangers in New York on December 19, 1943, and two nights later a 7–1 loss to the Black Hawks in Chicago. Then, on December 23, 1943, he was loaned to the Rangers on an emergency basis in a game against the Wings, playing only twenty minutes in a 5–3 Detroit win at home. In that first game, he was just seventeen years, thirty-eight days old.

BODNAR'S QUICK FIRST GOAL

THE RECORD On October 30, 1943, Gus Bodnar scored a goal just fifteen seconds into his first shift, netting the fastest first goal in NHL history.

HOW IT WAS DONE After playing for several years for the Fort William Rangers, Bodnar was brought up to the Leafs to fill in due to a lack of players during the war. Not big, he nonetheless had a sweet touch around the net, and in the first game of the 1943–44 season against the New York Rangers, he scored on his first shift. The Leafs won the game, 5–2, before 11,654 fans at Maple Leaf Gardens, a game that started with a ceremonial faceoff between the two team captains—Bob Davidson of the Leafs and Ott Heller of the Rangers. Ontario premier George Drew dropped the puck.

The *New York Times* had this to say about Bodnar in its game story the following morning: "The Leafs seized command with a goal in the first minute of play by Gus Bodnar, twenty-year-old Army reject from Fort William, who centres Toronto's first line." Bodnar knocked in a loose puck off a scramble in front of goalie Ken McAuley, a rookie in his own right who faced fifty-two shots in the loss. Bodnar played on a line with Bob Davidson and Elwyn Morris.

Davidson and Morris got the assists on Bodnar's historic goal, and the rookie scored again early in the third period to give the Leafs a 4–0 lead. Davidson and Babe Pratt assisted on that goal which also put Bodnar in select company as a player who scored twice in his first NHL game.

Incredibly, there were a total of twelve players in the game who were making their NHL debuts or were raw rookies, five for the Leafs and seven for the Rangers. For the Leafs, the newcomers were Bodnar, Morris, Eric Prentice, Red Carr, and Ross Johnstone. New to the Blueshirts were goalie Ken McAuley, Tom Dewar, Jackie Mann, Bill Warwick (who played a single game the previous year), Archie Fraser, Don Raleigh, and Jack McDonald.

WHY IT WON'T BE EQUALLED

More than 7,000 players have appeared in the NHL, and in the nearly seven decades since Bodnar's feat no one has bettered him yet, though a few have come close. Of course, it is a record that could be broken tomorrow or the day after, but whether a superstar making his first appearance or a one-game wonder happy to be in the league, no player has scored his

OTHER FAST STARTS

There have been many great and memorable first games for NHLers over the years even if no one else has managed to equal Bodnar's feat. Several players have scored on their first shot or first shift, including Mario Lemieux. He stripped Boston's Ray Bourque of the puck at the Pittsburgh blue-line, roared the length of the ice on a breakaway, and beat goalie Pete Peeters with an all-star deke. Far less famously, but equally impressive, Montreal's Andrew Cassels also scored on his first shift and first shot.

THE SECOND AND THIRD FASTEST

Danny Gare came mighty close to Bodnar's record when he made his NHL debut at the start of the 1974–75 season with Buffalo. The game was October 10, 1974, and Gare was in the starting lineup. Just eighteen seconds after the opening faceoff, he beat Gilles Gilbert for his first career goal. Right behind Gare is Russian star Alexander Mogilny. When he made his debut with Buffalo on October 5, 1989, he wasted little time in getting his first NHL goal, just twenty seconds after he stepped on the ice for the first time in a game against the Quebec Nordiques.

DANNY GARE.

first goal as quickly, whether off a rink-length dash or a deflection off his butt. There is both luck and timing needed to score so quickly, as most players simply want to get the first shift over with without having a goal scored against him.

RECORDS FOREVER

DEREK STEPAN SCORED A HAT TRICK IN HIS FIRST NHL GAME.

GREAT DEBUTS While Bodnar scored quickly in his first game, he is not one of an equally incredible group of players. Only four times has a player scored a hat trick in his first game—Alex Smart, Real Cloutier, Fabian Brunnstrom, and Derek Stepan. Stepan did it most recently, October 9, 2010, and at twenty years of age he was also the youngest. He should be leery of the feat, though, as Smart, who did it first, in 1943, faded quickly, as did Brunnstrom, who did it at the start of the 2008–09 season. Only Cloutier had a decent career after such a fast start, but he did it in 1979 after several years in the WHA, not really a true rookie.

MOSIENKO'S BLACK JACK HAT TRICK

THE RECORD On March 23, 1952, the final day of the 1951–52 season, Bill Mosienko scored three goals in just twenty-one seconds during Chicago's 7–6 win over the Rangers at Madison Square Garden in New York.

HOW IT WAS DONE Mosienko's feat came early in the third period. He scored at 6:09, again at 6:20, and finally at 6:30. All goals came against goalie Lorne Anderson. Just forty-five seconds later, Mosienko hit the post, missing a fourth quick goal by inches. The record shattered the previous mark of three goals in sixty-four seconds, set by Carl Liscombe of Detroit in 1938. Mosienko even bettered the NHL's record for fastest three goals by one *team*, previously set by the Montreal Maroons in 1932, who scored three in twenty-four seconds.

The record was announced over the p.a. system and received a great ovation from the scant 3,254 patrons in attendance. Anderson had played almost all of the season with a minor-league team, the New York Rovers, joining the Rangers for only the last three games of the NHL season. The game was played without a penalty being assessed to either team by referee George Gravel, and Mosienko's goals started a remarkable rally.

Gus Bodnar, who holds the record for the fastest goal to start his career, also holds the record for the fastest three assists, thanks to Mosienko. Bodnar assisted on all three goals, giving him the record. Bert Olmstead assisted on all of Jean Beliveau's goals when Le Gros Bil scored a hat trick in forty-four seconds, and as result he is in second place for the fastest three assists.

The Hawks were trailing 6–2 early in the third but thanks to "Wee Willie" Mosienko's hat trick and two late goals from Sid Finney—the last, and game winner, at 19:22—the Hawks managed a 7–6 win. Mosienko played on a line with Gus Bodnar and George Gee. The Black Hawks finished the season in last place in the regular-season standings with just forty-three points while the Rangers, in fifth, had fifty-nine. Neither team made the playoffs.

WHY IT WON'T BE EQUALLED Of course, it's physically possible to score three goals faster. If two players have scored twice in four seconds, there's nothing to suggest a third goal couldn't be added four seconds later. But consider first that a coach often changes lines after a goal. And, if a team gets two goals quickly, he'll almost certainly change lines. But even if he doesn't, time has proved Mosienko's feat is one for the ages.

The next fastest hat trick belongs to Jean Beliveau who, at forty-four seconds, is practically lethargic by comparison. Beliveau got his three in 1955 while the Habs were on a two-man advantage. This was the last year minor penalties had to be served in full, a rule change motivated in large measure by this very situation when a potent Montreal power play could pretty much clinch a game through one successful advantage. Beliveau scored at 0:42, 1:08, and 1:26 of the second period, all with the two-man advantage. Mosienko, by comparison, scored all his goals with both teams at full strength.

FASTEST TWO GOALS Only two players have ever scored goals four seconds apart. Nels Stewart of the Montreal Maroons was the first, in 1931, when he scored at 8:24 and 8:28 of the third period in a game against the Boston Bruins. The record stood alone for sixty-four years until little-known Deron Quint did same on December 15, 1995, while playing for the Winnipeg Jets. He connected at 7:51 and 7:55 of the second period against the Edmonton Oilers in a game won by the Jets, 9–4.

In Quint's case, not one but both goals were lucky. The first came when his long shot tipped off an Oilers' stick past goalie Joaquin Gage, making only his third NHL start and first in the quirky Winnipeg Arena. The second, right off the ensuing faceoff, was even crazier. Alexei Zhamnov won the draw right to Quint, and he fired the puck into the Edmonton end along the glass. But as Gage went behind the net to play it, the puck hit a stanchion and bounced right into the goal.

DERON QUINT.

FASTEST FOUR GOALS

While Mosienko's feat is incredible—almost impossible—another record is likely never to be broken, either. In the first period of a Washington–Tampa Bay game on February 5, 1994, Peter Bondra of the Capitals scored four goals in just 4:12. He beat goalie Daren Puppa at 14:44, 15:59, 16:50, and 18:56, an extraordinary burst of production never matched before or since. Bondra later scored a fifth goal in the second period but was held off the scoresheet in the third period as he tried to reach six or even seven.

PETER BONDRA.

LEAFS USE THREE GOALIES IN ONE GAME

THE RECORD On April 3, 1966, coach Punch Imlach tweaked the rulebook to allow three goalies to play in one game. Johnny Bower played the first period; Terry Sawchuk played the second; and, Bruce Gamble played the third period. Toronto and Detroit played to a 3–3 tie at the Olympia.

GOALIE BRUCE GAMBLE MAKES A SAVE IN THE MAPLE LEAFS' NET.

HOW IT WAS DONE The final game of the season was meaningless in the standings to both Toronto and Detroit. The Leafs were in third place, well ahead of Detroit and far enough behind second-place Chicago that the result didn't matter. Ditto for Detroit, well ahead of fifth place Boston and assured of a playoff spot.

Imlach wanted to give his new goalie, Bruce Gamble, some playing time and wanted to rest his veterans for the first round of the playoffs against Montreal, so he used all three goalies. However, a team is permitted to use only two in a game, the starter and his backup. The only exception is if the starter is injured, the team is permitted to dress a third goalie so the backup has, well, a backup. After the first period, Imlach claimed Bower, who played shutout hockey for the opening twenty minutes, had "the flu" and would not be able to continue.

Backup Terry Sawchuk played the middle period and allowed one goal while Gamble came out of

TORONTO MAPLE LEAFS ™

JASON ALLISON AS BACKUP

The top junior player in Canada in 1993–94, Allison led Canada to gold at the World U20 (Junior) Championship in 1994 and 1995. His peripatetic career took him to Nashville at one point, and in a game on December 13, 2005, in Sunrise, Florida, he was forced to dress as the backup goalie for the Predators. During the pre-game warmup, starter Chris Mason pulled a groin, forcing backup Brian Finley into action. Finley was making his NHL debut, and with no other goalie near at hand and the Predators required to dress two goalies, coach Barry Trotz turned to defenceman Allison, who sat in full goalie equipment at the end of the bench but didn't see game action.

the stands to dress as Sawchuk's backup to start the second. Unfortunately, Sawchuk suffered a groin injury trying to make the save on Norm Ullman's goal—and was unable to come out for the third period. Miraculously, Bower was healthy enough by the start of the third period—when third goalie Gamble was in the net—to assume coaching duties while Imlach watched the rest of the game from the gondola! Said referee-in-chief Scotty Morrison: "Imlach was within his rights to dress and play the third goaltender when the other two became incapacitated."

TERRY SAWCHUK WAS ONE OF THREE GOALIES TO PLAY TWENTY MINUTES IN A GAME FOR THE LEAFS.

For those who think using three goalies in a game is odd, get ready for another strange Maple Leafs game, played on March 30, 1969, at Madison Square Garden. The record shows that the Leafs lost the game 4–0, and it's probably a good thing they did. Imlach had considered the possibility of a coach changing his goalies like his forwards and defencemen, putting them in and taking them off after regular "shifts." He thought this was the way of the future, and for one night he experimented with Bower and Gamble, taking them out and putting them back in every five minutes or so! Had the Leafs won this night, he might well have continued this unorthodox practice, but they lost and the test ended after sixty minutes.

WHY IT WON'T BE EQUALLED Never before or since have three goalies played twenty minutes each for one team in a single game. A coach has never had need to use three in this manner, and at no time has both the starter and backup been injured seriously enough to warrant the use of a third goalie. Many times a coach has made two goaltending changes—pull the starter; reinsert him later—but a third goalie, all of whom play a full period? Never. No reason.

JOHNNY BOWER JUGGLES A SHOT WHILE MAKING THE SAVE.

AN EXTRAORDINARY THIRD GOALIE

Actually, there was an NHL game in which three goalies did dress for the same team. The date was December 12, 2008, and the location was the Verizon Center in Washington. Jose Theodore, the team's number-one goalie, injured his hip flexor the morning of the game. His backup, Brent Johnson, was then ready to play that night against Ottawa, and the Capitals recalled their top goalie from the farm team in Hershey, Semyon Varlamov. But the Bears were playing a road game in San Antonio, Texas, and Varlamov couldn't get to D.C. in time for the start of the game.

The Caps then signed Brett Leonhardt, the team's website producer, to a one-game amateur contract. Leonhardt dressed, took the warmup, and sat at the end of the bench for most of the first period until Varlamov arrived. At six-foot-seven, Leonhardt would have been the tallest goalie ever to play in the NHL had Johnson been forced to leave the game. Leonhardt, an Ontarian, had played Division III NCAA hockey and had periodically taken part in practice when the Caps needed an extra goalie.

BRETT LEONHARDT DRESSED BUT DIDN'T PLAY FOR
THE CAPS IN AN EMERGENCY SITUATION.

THE FIVE EASIEST GOALS EVER SCORED

THE RECORD On April 5, 1970, the Chicago Black Hawks scored five empty-net goals during the final seven minutes of a game against Montreal.

HOW IT WAS DONE The 1969–70 season represented the third and final season wherein the East Division consisted of the Original Six teams and the West Division the six expansion teams of 1967. The top four teams in each division made the playoffs, and these four played best of seven series to determine who went to the Final. This assured the Cup was contested by one old team and one new team.

In 1969–70, the tie-breaking system for playoff qualification was simple. The team with the greater number of goals earned the higher placing if two teams had the same number of points in the standings. This created a problem for the Montreal Canadiens on the final day of the regular season, April 5. Prior to the teams' final games of the seventy-six-game schedule, the Rangers had ninety points and the Habs had ninety-two.

Montreal played Chicago, the first place team in the East, at night while the Blueshirts were scheduled to play Detroit that afternoon. As important, the Habs had scored 242 goals while the Rangers just 237. On

BOBBY HULL (MIDDLE) GOES UP AGAINST THE HABS IN ANOTHER CHICAGO-MONTREAL CLASSIC.

the morning of April 5, everything favoured Montreal advancing to the playoffs and eliminating the Rangers in the process. But then all hell broke loose.

For starters, the Rangers hammered the Red Wings by a 9–5 score, killing two birds with one stone. First, they moved into a tie with Montreal with ninety-two points, but they also upped their goals total to 246. The Rangers even pulled goalie Ed Giacomin late in the game to try to score more. After all, giving up empty netters didn't matter; only goals scored mattered.

By dinner time, the Canadiens realized they had to either win their game against Chicago or score at least five goals in a losing cause (so that, even with the same number of points, they would have more goals). Things seemed to be alright when Yvan Cournoyer scored in the first period and Jean Beliveau early in the second, but the Hawks took a 3–2 lead into the final period. The situation got worse when Pit Martin scored two goals by the midway mark to make it a 5–2 score.

At that point, Habs coach Claude Ruel went into panic mode. A loss seemed pretty certain now, so the Habs had to focus solely on scoring. It didn't matter if they allowed twenty goals—they had to score five, and they had only two so far. And so, Ruel pulled goalie Rogie Vachon with nearly half a period to play, hoping the extended man advantage would produce three more goals. It didn't turn out like that.

PULLING THE GOALIE

It is believed the first documented instance of a team pulling a goalie for an extra attacker occurred on January 21, 1932, at the Forum in Montreal. Trailing the Habs 2–1, Toronto coach Dick Irvin pulled goalie Lorne Chabot, but the manoeuvre backfired. Aurel Joliat scored at 19:48 into the empty cage to seal the win.

BILLY SMITH OF THE NEW YORK ISLANDERS.

FIRST GOALIE GOAL The most common reason for pulling a goalie is a delayed penalty because as soon as the other team touches the puck, play is dead. Once in a blue moon, however, the tactic backfires and a team accidentally scores into its own goal. This happened most famously on November 28, 1979, when the Islanders were playing the Colorado Rockies. The Rockies had a delayed penalty, pulled their goalie, and had their own Rob Ramage fire an inaccurate pass that went all the way down the ice and into his own net. The last Islanders player to touch the puck got credit for the goal, and that happened to be goalie Billy Smith, the first NHL goalie credited with a goal.

Chicago's Eric Nesterenko scored the first goal into the empty Montreal net at 12:27 to make it 6–2, but still Vachon sat on the bench. Cliff Koroll made it 7–2; Bobby and Dennis Hull made it 9–2; and, Gerry Pinder added a fifth empty netter at 19:57 to make it an even 10–2. The Habs failed to qualify for the playoffs, falling three goals short. The result was significant for two other reasons. It marked the first time no Canadian team had qualified for the Stanley Cup playoffs, and it marked Chicago's rise from last to first in one season, a feat that had never been accomplished previously.

WHY IT WON'T BE EQUALLED Of course, this game exposed the extreme flaw of the qualification rule, and the NHL changed it that very summer. Goal differential began to be used, and now, with shootouts leaving no games tied, head-to-head is the single determining tiebreak between two teams. There is no need ever to pull a goalie for such an extended time, and as such no team could possibly be in a position to score or allow as many empty netters again.

THE RUSHING GOALIE

While pulling the goalie didn't become common until the 1960s, one goalie in particular tried to help his team late in games by joining the rush. Charlie Rayner, who played for the Rangers between 1945 and 1953, was the game's first wandering goalie, often stickhandling to the other team's blueline to help out on offence. The NHL later prohibited goalies from crossing centre ice, a rule still in place.

A NEW STRATEGY FOR PULLING THE GOALIE
Although this has never been tried in the NHL, the move has been used successfully elsewhere, most often in the top German league, DEL. A team gains a two-man advantage and pulls the goalie to create a six-on-three situation. The tactic is considered foolproof because, with twice as many men on the ice, what are the chances the other team will even touch the puck let alone control it long enough to fire an accurate shot the length of the ice?

Germany's coach Uwe Krupp, who scored the Cup-winning goal for Colorado in 1996, tried it against Team USA at the Deutschland Cup in 2009. Trailing 3–0 midway through the second period, and desperate to change the course of the game, Krupp's team had a two-man advantage thanks to two quick penalties. He pulled his goalie, and with the three extra men, scored. On May 10, 1996, Las Vegas coach Chris McSorley (brother of Marty) successfully used the tactic in an IHL game. While the move is best tried out of desperation, McSorley did it in a 1–1 game. His team scored and eventually won in overtime, 3–2.

SITTLER GETS DOUBLE DIGITS—IN ONE GAME

THE RECORD On February 7, 1976, Darryl Sittler recorded ten points in a single game, leading Toronto to an 11–4 win over Boston at Maple Leaf Gardens. His totals included six goals and four assists.

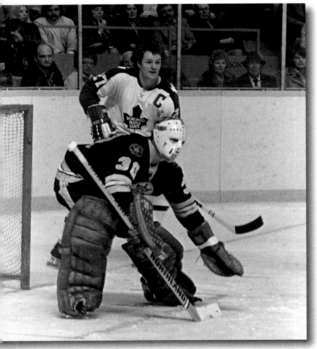

HOW IT WAS DONE No one could have imagined such a night. The Leafs were a very good team in 1975–76, and Sittler was the team's captain and best player. Boston, a very good opponent, was in town, but coach Don Cherry started Dave Reece in goal, not Gilles Gilbert, who was injured, or his normal backup, Gerry Cheevers, who was just retuning to the NHL from the WHA and not ready to play. (This also helps explain why Reece was never pulled, allowing all eleven goals.)

Sittler had two assists in the first period as Toronto took a 2–1 lead. So far, nothing special. But in the second period, all hell broke loose. The teams combined to score nine goals, the Leafs getting six, with Sittler having a hand in five (3 goals, 2 assists). That gave him seven points. During the second intermission, Leafs' publicity man Stan Obodiac came into the dressing room and told Sittler that the record for points in a game was eight, a record jointly held by Maurice Richard and Bert Olmstead.

Well, wouldn't you know that Sittler tied the record early in the third, eclipsed it midway through, and then topped it off with his tenth point late in the third on his luckiest play yet. Behind the Boston net, he fired a pass out to Errol Thompson in the slot that bounced off the skate of Brad Park and past a helpless Reece. Ten points—and Reece never played another NHL game.

WHY IT WON'T BE EQUALLED   Only two players ever had eight points before Sittler's big night, and since then another ten players have had eight. It's a list of mostly great players, from Wayne Gretzky to Mario Lemieux, both of whom did it twice, to Bryan Trottier and Peter Stastny. Bernie Nicholls and Anton Stastny also hit eight, as did two defence-men, little-known Tom Bladon and Hall of Famer Paul Coffey. If in all the tens of thousands of hockey games ever played, in all the eras with various rules and goal-tenders and offence and great stars, no one can even get nine points, Sittler's record is as safe as can be.

International hockey has produced three ten-point games, and two were from the same game. On April 11, 1973, at the fortieth World Championship, in Moscow, the Soviet Union crushed Poland 20–0. In that game both Boris Mikhailov and Vladimir Petrov had ten points, the former accruing seven goals and three assists and the latter five goals and assists. Also, in a World U20 (Junior) Championship game on December 20, 1992, Sweden ham-mered Japan by a 20–1 count in Gavle, Sweden. Peter Forsberg led the attack with three goals and seven assists. In all cases, though, the opponent paled beside Sittler's feat against a top Boston team.

BOBBY ORR CONDUCTS THE CEREMONIAL FACEOFF PRIOR TO THE CHALLENGE CUP IN 1979 WITH SOVIET BORIS MIKHAILOV AND CANADIAN BOBBY CLARKE.

1976 SITTLER'S GREATEST YEAR

The year 1976 was the pinnacle of Sittler's career in many ways. After this ten-point game, he scored five goals in a playoff game to tie a record that has yet to be bettered. The achievement came on April 22, 1976, in an 8–5 home win over the Philadelphia Flyers. Then, in September that year, Sittler scored the overtime goal to give Canada victory at the inaugural Canada Cup, his finest international moment.

THE HISTORIC GAME SUMMARY
Boston 4 at Toronto 11

First Period
1. Toronto, McDonald (Sittler) 6:19
2. Toronto, Turnbull (Sittler, Thompson) 7:01
3. Boston, Ratelle (Schmautz) 16:51
Penalties: Sims (BOS—minor, major) & Boutette (TOR—minor, major), 13:00

Second Period
4. Toronto, Sittler (McDonald, Salming) 2:56
5. Toronto, Salming (Sittler) 3:33
6. Boston, Schmautz (Bucyk, Ratelle) 5:19
7. Toronto, Sittler (unassisted) 8:12
8. Toronto, Sittler (Ferguson, Valiquette) 10:27
9. Boston, Bucyk (Ratelle, Schmautz) 11:06
10. Toronto, Ferguson (Garland, Hammarstrom) 11:40
11. Toronto, Salming (McDonald, Sittler) 13:57
12. Boston, Ratelle (Gibson, Schmautz) 14:35
Penalties: Park (BOS) 3:29, Sheppard (BOS) 8:45, Ferguson (TOR) 16:27, Forbes (BOS) 19:44

Third Period
13. Toronto, Sittler (Salming, Thompson) 0:44
14. Toronto, Sittler (Thompson) 9:27
15. Toronto, Sittler (McDonald) 16:35
Penalties: Salming (TOR) 3:46, Edestrand (BOS) 9:50

Shots on Goal
Boston	11	9	12	32
Toronto	9	21	10	40

In Goal
Boston—Reece
Toronto—Thomas

Attendance: 16, 485

DARRYL SITTLER SCORED THE WINNING GOAL AGAINST CZECH
GOALIE VLADIMIR DZURILLA IN THE 1976 CANADA CUP.

BLADON IS A PERFECT PLUS-10

THE RECORD On December 11, 1977, the Philadelphia Flyers beat the Cleveland Barons 11–1. Defenceman Tom Bladon had a plus-minus of plus-10, the highest ever for any one game.

HOW IT WAS DONE Calculating plus-minus is easy. A player is credited with one "plus" every time he is on the ice when his team scores an even-strength or short-handed goal. He is credited with one "minus" when he is on the ice for an even-strength or short-handed goal against. Bladon earned his plus-10 mostly by scoring four goals and adding four assists in the game, a record for a defenceman (later equaled by Paul Coffey, in 1986), and being on the ice for two other Flyers' goals. He also set a points record for the Flyers and became the first Flyers defenceman to record even three goals. In fact, the only Flyers' goal scored without Bladon on the ice was their fifth, netted by Rick MacLeish early in the second period.

The Barons scored their only goal on the power play, so no one on the ice at the time got credit as either a plus or minus for that goal. What is unique, though, is that the Flyers scored all their eleven goals at even strength.

His teammates called him "Sparkie," and his career night began late in the first period when his shot from the right point beat Gary Edwards. The Flyers got two late goals in the period, and Bladon assisted on both. He had two goals in the second period to give him the hat trick, sending the Spectrum crowd into a frenzy. Early in the third another point shot went in past Gilles Meloche, who came into the game for Edwards when the score was 8–0. Bladon added two more assists in the period to finish with eight points on the night.

THE 2010–11 SEASON

To put Orr's plus-124 season record in context, consider that the best plus-minus in 2010–11 belonged to giant Boston defenceman Zdeno Chara, who was all of plus-33. Of the top eleven leaders that year, eight were defencemen. The worst plus-minus belonged to veteran Ottawa defenceman Chris Phillips who was a disastrous minus-35. David Booth of Florida was minus-31 and Phillips's teammate Erik Carlsson was a minus-30.

"It seemed like every time I touched the puck, it went in," he said after. That final assist, though, might have been a goal. It came off another point shot that was tipped in front by Bill Barber, and some fans thought it might have gone in without assistance. If it had, Bladon would have ended the evening with five goals, tying Ian Turnbull of the Leafs for most goals by a defenceman in a game.

"I'm not trying to be modest," Bladon explained, "but I don't think records are that big of a thing. I'd much rather win the Stanley Cup. If I'd really wanted that fifth goal, I could have shot high. But it's easier to score if you keep it low, so maybe somebody can tip it in." Barber did just that.

BEST RATING IN A YEAR AND CAREER Having an outstanding plus-minus over a long period of time is reserved for the superstars of the game. Plus-10 in a game is a fluke; only the best of the best can sustain a high figure over a season or a career. Bobby Orr holds the single-season record of plus-124 (in 1970–71), but more incredibly he led the league in plus-minus six times in his nine full NHL seasons. Wayne Gretzky led the league four times, and only three other players have led twice (John LeClair, Chris Pronger, and Larry Robinson).

Robinson is the career leader at plus-730 thanks to the combination of a lengthy career and playing for a great team for so many seasons (Montreal). Orr is second all-time at plus-597, obviously lower given that he played half the total games Robinson played. Although not exclusively so, the plus-minus favours defencemen (high and low) because they usually get more ice time than forwards. A top blue-liner will get, for instance, thirty minutes a game, and a top forward perhaps twenty-three minutes.

LARRY ROBINSON.

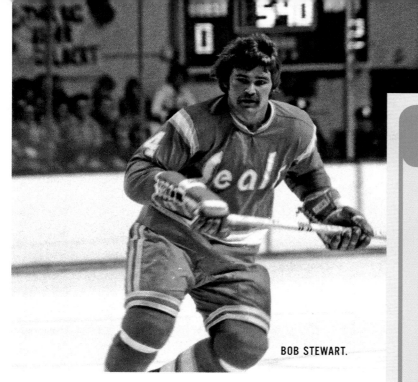

BOB STEWART.

WORST PLUS-MINUS

More than one hundred players have had a one-game plus-minus of minus-7, but no one has gone so low as minus-8. The worst career stat belongs to Bob Stewart. He started his career with the mighty Boston Bruins in 1971–72, the year they won the Cup for the second time in three years. But long before Orr, Espo, and Bucyk hoisted the prize, Stewart was traded to the California Golden Seals. In his eight games with Boston he didn't record a point but was a plus-3. Unbelievably, he was a minus player every year for the rest of his nine-year career. That 1971–72 season had him a minus-11 in sixteen games with the Seals, and in subsequent years with that team, Cleveland, St. Louis, and Pittsburgh he was a cumulative minus-250.

WHY IT WON'T BE EQUALLED In 2010–11, there was only one game in 1,230 in which a team scored ten goals or more. St. Louis beat Detroit 10–3 on March 30, 2011. In that game, two Blues had a rating of plus-3, Roman Polak and Nikita Nikitin. One Red Wings player, forward Jiri Hudler, was a minus-4. Two of the Blues' ten goals came on the power play. For a player to approach Bladon's mark, he first has to be in a game in which his team scores at least ten goals, a rare game, indeed. Then, the team scoring the ten must do so all at even strength, a near impossibility. And, finally, the player must be on ice for each and every goal his team scores, an even more absurd possibility. Oh, and he must also not be on the ice when the other team scores. Every year, the league's thirty teams play a total of 1,230 games, and no one has come close to Bladon's record.

SABRES SCORE NINE IN A PERIOD

THE RECORD On March 19, 1981, the Buffalo Sabres scored nine goals against Toronto in under sixteen minutes, the most goals ever scored in one period.

ANDRE SAVARD LED A RECORD SCORING SPREE FOR THE SABRES.

HOW IT WAS DONE Although the Leafs were at the bottom of the Adams Division and the Sabres at the top, no one could have predicted the events that were about to unfold in the second period of this game near the end of the regular season. In fact, there was only one goal in the opening period, an early power-play goal from John van Boxmeer that staked the hometown Sabres to a slim, 1–0, lead.

But Gilbert Perreault made it 2–0 at 4:27 of the second period, and midway through the period the Sabres scored three more goals in two and a half minutes. Another burst saw the Leafs score three of the four goals they would get that game, but the Sabres ended the period with four more tallies in less than four minutes. By the time teams went to the dressing room for the second intermission, Buffalo had a 10–3 lead and had scored nine goals in fifteen minutes and twenty seconds. The combined twelve goals also set a record tied four years later by Edmonton and Chicago. Incredibly, Michel Larocque allowed all ten goals for the Leafs through forty minutes, but he was replaced by Jiri Crha for the final period.

Larocque was playing in only his fourth game for the Leafs after coming to the team in a trade with Montreal. He had won the previous three, but left red-faced after this horrible period. The teams also set two other records in the period, the Sabres for most points by one team in a period (23) and most points by both teams in a period (31).

THE OTHER TWELVE-GOAL PERIOD

Edmonton and Chicago scored six goals each in the second period of another memorable game, December 11, 1985. Won by the Oilers, 12–9, the game also tied a record for most goals combined in a game, first set in 1920 by Toronto St. Pats and the Canadiens (Montreal won the game, 14–7). Wayne Gretzky had seven assists in that game, one of three times in his career he achieved that record (tied with Billy Taylor, who had done it first, in 1947). In fact, of the four highest-scoring games of all time, the Oilers are involved in three of them (excepting the 1920 classic).

THE FINAL TALLY Both Gilbert Perreault and Andre Savard had hat tricks for the Sabres in the game, but Savard also had three assists for a six-point night, the best of his career. Perreault had one assist for four points. The rest of the scoring looked like this:

Rod Seiling and John van Boxmeer had one goal and three assists each.
Danny Gare and Derek Smith had two goals and an assist each.
Tony McKegney and Larry Playfair had three assists each.
Craig Ramsay had a goal and assist.
Pierre Hamel had a goal.
Jim Schoenfeld, Lindy Ruff, and Bill Hajt had one assist each.

For Toronto, Darryl Sittler had two goals and Wilf Paiement and Ian Turnbull had three assists each. Borje Salming had one assist. Terry Martin and Rod Sedlbauer had the other Leafs' goals.

In the early days of international hockey it was common for Canada and the United States to win games by fifteen or twenty goals. As recently as the 1956 Olympics, for instance, Canada scored eleven goals in a period against Austria in a 23–0 win. In 1920, the first time hockey was played at the Olympics, the Americans scored fifteen goals against Switzerland in one half (games were two periods of twenty minutes each).

At the World Championship, Canada has scored at least thirteen goals in a period on four occasions, most famously in 1949. That year, Canada scored eighteen times in one, twenty-minute period against Denmark in a 47–0 win, the most lop-sided score in top level international hockey history.

WHY IT WON'T BE EQUALLED A team has scored eight goals in a period eight times, but only the Sabres have scored nine. Of course, this is a very beatable record in the sense that there is almost no limit to the number of goals a team can score in twenty minutes, but if no team has equaled this mark over ninety-five years and tens of thousands of games, it isn't likely to happen now in an era when nine goals in sixty minutes is rare, when goaltending is as good as it's ever been, and when coaching systems do not allow for such scoring binges.

TM

CANADA (IN WHITE) SCORED GOALS AT WILL AT THE 1924
OLYMPIC WINTER GAMES IN CHAMONIX, FRANCE.

IMPOSSIBLE—BOSTON AND ST. LOUIS SCORE TWO SECONDS APART

THE RECORD On December 19, 1987, Ken Linseman of Boston scored at 19:50 of the third period. Doug Gilmour of St. Louis then scored at 19:52, the fastest two goals ever scored.

DOUG GILMOUR.

HOW IT WAS DONE The game summary shows that St. Louis beat Boston 7–5 in a game at the Boston Garden before 11,775 fans. The Bruins took a 3–0 lead before the game was eight minutes old, but the Blues rallied for a goal later in the period and then scored the only three goals of the second period to lead 4–3 after forty minutes. The Bruins tied it 4–4 early in the third, but St. Louis went ahead on a Tony McKegney goal at 4:54. The rest of the period was uneventful until the very end.

The Bruins pulled goalie Doug Keans in the final minute to try to tie the game, but Gino Cavallini scored into an empty net at 19:18 to make it 6–4. Game over, right? Wrong. Ken Linseman scored for the Bruins at 19:50 to make it 6–5, so with just ten seconds left in the game, Boston coach Terry O'Reilly kept Keans on the bench for the faceoff at centre ice, again in the hopes of tying the game with only ten seconds left and a faceoff at centre. Doug Gilmour of St. Louis won the draw by shooting the puck directly into the empty Boston net at 19:52, just two seconds after Cavallini's goal.

Gilmour won the draw cleanly and shot the puck in a perfectly straight line into the goal before any Bruins player had even reacted to the faceoff. What makes this such an amazing play is not

FASTEST TWO GOALS, ONE PLAYER

Twice in NHL history has a player scored two goals in four seconds, the occurrences separated by decades. In both instances empty-net goals were not involved, making this record perhaps all the more impressive. On January 3, 1931, Nels Stewart scored at 8:24 and 8:28 of the third period to help the Montreal Maroons defeat the Boston Bruins, 5–3. That record stood alone for sixty-four years until Deron Quint scored at 7:51 and 7:55 of the second period to help Winnipeg crush Edmonton, 9–4.

NELS STEWART.

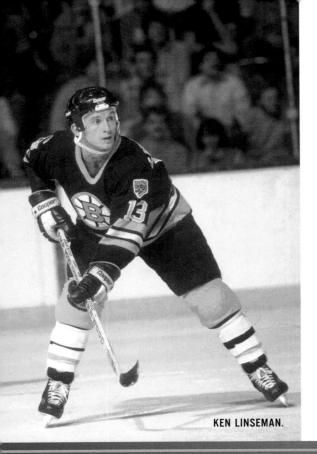

KEN LINSEMAN.

that Gilmour scored into the empty net, but that he deliberately fired the puck off the draw from centre into the net. After all, how many times during a season does a centreman taking a faceoff at centre ice record a shot on goal from the faceoff, even with the goalie in goal? Never. The previous record for two goals was four seconds, accomplished many times.

WHY IT WON'T BE EQUALLED It is virtually impossible to score two seconds after a faceoff at centre ice. That it has been done once in the hundreds of thousands of NHL games is incredible; for it to happen again? Never. After all, to watch the play on YouTube, one can see it's not possible for the puck to get from centre ice to the empty goal any faster (unless the timekeeper is slow to start the game clock).

THREE IN FIFTEEN Another extraordinary speed record occurred in a game between the Minnesota North Stars and New York Rangers on February 10, 1983. Teams combined to score three goals in just fifteen seconds late in the second period, none involving an empty net.

Mark Pavelich of the Rangers scored at 19:18 on a power play to start the record, taking a Ron Duguay pass in the slot and banging the puck in past Don Beaupre. This was a huge goal for Pavelich because he had arranged for two busloads of family and friends from his hometown of Eveleth, Minnesota, to attend the game. Nine seconds later, teammate Ron Greschner scored at 19:27, getting to the rebound off a Barry Beck shot before anyone else. It was his first goal of the season in just his third game, having missed the last year with a serious back injury.

Just six seconds later, Willi Plett of the North Stars scored again when his shot from the top of the faceoff circle beat Eddie Mio in the Rangers' goal. The previous record was eighteen seconds, which had been done twice, in 1963 (Montreal–Rangers) and 1976 (Oakland–Buffalo). After the game, representatives from the Hockey Hall of Fame asked Plett for his stick to honour the new record.

JIM DOWD OF THE MINNESOTA WILD.

FASTEST TWO GOALS, ONE TEAM

The Minnesota Wild scored twice in three seconds on January 1, 2004. Jim Dowd scored at 19:44 of the third period, and Richard Park scored at 19:47. The Wild won the home game, 4–2, over Chicago. The quick chain of events started when Dowd scored with 15.5 seconds left on the clock. The team had been struggling badly, with just four wins in the previous sixteen games, and it had blown a 2–0 lead in this game. The Hawks immediately called a timeout, and when the faceoff took place at centre ice, goalie Craig Anderson was on the bench for an extra attacker. Park won the draw against Brett McLean and fired the puck eighty-eight feet into the open net just three seconds after Dowd had scored.

The NHL doesn't keep count of tenths of seconds in its game summaries, and while newspapers noted Dowd's goal with 15.5 seconds remaining, reports weren't as precise for Park's goal. The time in the final minute is always rounded up to the next second, even if the clock shows .1 (i.e., a goal scored with 4.1 seconds left is recorded as 19:55). So, the actual playing time between the two goals could be anywhere from 2.5 seconds (if there were exactly 13 seconds left in the game), or 3.4 seconds (if there were 12.1 seconds remaining). Either way, it's a record for fastest two goals by one team.

MARIO SCORES EVERY WHICH WAY

THE RECORD On December 31, 1988, Pittsburgh captain Mario Lemieux scored five goals in a game, one in every possible game situation—even strength, power play, short-handed, penalty shot, and empty net.

HOW IT WAS DONE It was New Year's Eve, 1988, and Mario Lemieux was at the very height of his powers. In a home game against New Jersey, he had a hat trick by the midway point of the first period and finished with five goals and three assists in an 8–6 win. The eight-point game gave him 104 on the season and the lead in the season's scoring race.

He opened the scoring for the Penguins with an even strength goal at 4:17, tying the game, 1–1. At 7:50 he took a nice outlet pass from Rob Brown while short-handed and beat Bob Sauve with a shot to give his team the lead. The Devils tied the game, but Mario rifled a shot in the short side from the left circle while Pittsburgh enjoyed a two-man advantage to restore the lead, 3–2. Early in the second he made a great pass to Brown for a 4–2 lead and his 100th point of the season. He got another helper on a Dan Quinn goal soon after. Midway through the period, Mario drew a penalty shot when goalie Chris Terreri tossed his stick at the puck Lemieux was in control of—an automatic penalty. Lemieux drilled the puck between the goalie's pads on the freebie for his fourth goal of the game. He added two more assists and then scored into the empty net at 19:59, his extraordinary night only one second away from being that much less significant.

WHY IT WON'T BE EQUALLED

Only twelve players have ever scored goals four different ways in a game, all of them missing the penalty shot. (Yanic Perreault, however, did manage to score a quintella with Trois-Rivieres in 1991 during his junior career in the QMJHL.) If you multiply the number of NHL games since 1917 by the number of players who have participated in those games, the NHL has seen probably more than two million man games come and go—and only once has a quintella been accomplished.

THE HISTORIC GOAL

There are three goals in Canadian hockey history that tower above all others: Paul Henderson's Summit Series winner on September 28, 1972, in Moscow; Mario Lemieux's series winner at the 1987 Canada Cup at Copps Coliseum in Hamilton on September 15; and, Sidney Crosby's golden goal on February 28, 2010, at the Vancouver Olympics. Mario's goal came off the rush and a perfect drop pass from Wayne Gretzky, late in game three of a best-of-three series in which all games were won, 6–5. The goal, at 18:34, was perhaps the most important of Lemieux's career. He led the tournament with eleven goals, nine of them assisted by number 99.

LEMIEUX CELEBRATES WITH GRETZKY AFTER COMBINING FORCES TO WIN THE 1987 CANADA CUP.

LEMIEUX (CENTRE) CONGRATULATES PAUL KARIYA ON HIS GOAL WHILE AL MACINNIS (LEFT) JOINS THE PARTY.

THE TOUCHLESS ASSIST

One of Mario Lemieux's most memorable plays came during the gold-medal game of the Olympics in Salt Lake City, on February 24, 2002. It started when he helped set up a goal by making a simple forward pass through centre. He moved the puck along the right wing to defenceman Chris Pronger, who stopped just inside the U.S. blue-line as the Canadian forwards went to the net. Pronger saw Lemieux going to the slot and whipped a pass to him, but Mario allowed the puck to go through his legs as he faked a shot. The feint fooled goalie Mike Richter, and coming in behind Lemieux was Paul Kariya who had a wide open net to shoot at. That first-period goal tied the score, 1–1, and Canada went on to win gold with a 5–2 win.

RECORDS FOREVER

On the afternoon of December 23, 2002, Pittsburgh radio host Mark Madden announced that he would donate 6,600 dollars to the Mario Lemieux Foundation if Lemieux ever scored a goal directly off a faceoff. Lemieux and the Penguins hosted the Buffalo Sabres that night. With the game tied 2–2 and a faceoff to the left of Sabres' goalie Mika Noronen, Lemieux did just what was asked of him midway through the third period. The linesman dropped the puck, and before Chris Gratton could get his stick on it, Lemieux snapped it past the stunned goalie at 13:10. It turned out to be the game-winning goal in a 5–2 decision.

Another way to think of it. How many games include a penalty-shot goal? Keep in mind that only about a third of penalty shots are successful. Now, what are the chances of the scorer also being good enough and lucky enough to add four more goals in a game, each in a different way? After all, there have been only fifty-four NHL games where a player has scored five or more goals in a game. The possibility of a player scoring a quintella certainly exists, but the chances are one in millions.

GOALIE JEFF REESE GETS THREE ASSISTS IN A GAME

THE RECORD Calgary Flames goalie Jeff Reese was credited with three assists on February 10, 1993, in a 13–1 home win over San Jose.

HOW IT WAS DONE Jeff Reese was, at best, a solid backup goalie during his eleven-year, 174-game career. He was drafted sixty-seventh overall by Toronto in 1984 and played the first five years of his career with the Leafs (1987–92) before being traded to Calgary in one of the biggest deals ever made. Going to the Flames with Reese were Gary Leeman, Michel Petit, Alexander Godynyuk, and Craig Berube for Doug Gilmour, Jamie Macoun, Ric Nattress, Kent Manderville, and Rick Walmsley. The deal was made on January 2, 1992, and Reese played twelve games in a backup role that year with the Flames and another four games in the playoffs. But midway through the next season, in a home game on February 10, 1993, he made history in a 13–1 walloping of the San Jose Sharks.

He drew an assist on a Robert Reichel goal midway through the first period and drew another on a Gary Roberts goal midway through the second period. At the halfway point of the final period, he got a third assist on another Reichel goal, becoming the first and only goalie to earn three points in a single game. The

Flames also set another record when they scored the fastest three goals to start a period, connecting three times in the first fifty-three seconds of the third period.

It was the sixteenth straight loss for the Sharks, playing in only their second NHL season, just one fewer than the worst losing streak in NHL history (seventeen by Washington, 1974–75). It also lowered their record to 6–47–2 after fifty-five games, the worst ever for an NHL team.

"A good choice of terms would be rock bottom," offered defenceman Doug Wilson. "The only way we can go from here is up. We've played good games, and we've played bad games, but this is the worst…They say you have to hit rock bottom before you come up, and this is rock bottom."

WHY IT WON'T BE EQUALLED Because of the dominance of the butterfly style of play, as well as the no-play trapezoid area behind the net and the speed of the game, goalies don't have the time or opportunity to handle the puck as they once did. The less they work with their defencemen, the less chance they have of earning an assist. Kari Lehtonen of Dallas led the league in goalie assists in 2010–11

GAME DETAILS

Crazy but true, despite losing 13–1 the Sharks actually held a 1–0 lead for half a period. Johan Garpenlov got the early goal, but before the end of the first the Flames had a 4–1 lead. Three goals in the second extended the lead and six more in the third put an exclamation point on the night's scoring binge. In addition to Reese, Robert Reichel was the star with a hat trick and three assists for six points. Theo Fleury also had a six-point night thanks to a goal and five assists. Both Gary Roberts and Gary Suter had two goals and two assists, while Ronald Stern had a hat trick.

MOST GOALIE ASSISTS, CAREER

Reese's great night, of course, was a fluke. No goalie can ever count on getting three assists in a game. At the same time, in the era of puck-handling goalies, there were many who became so involved in play it was only a matter of time before they accumulated some pretty decent points on their own.

Surprisingly, although he scored a goal in both the regular season and play-offs, Martin Brodeur is not a top assist leader. He has thirty-six career assists, but that is well back of the leader Tom Barrasso, who accumulated forty-eight during his career. Right behind him is Grant Fuhr with forty-six. Fuhr also holds the single-season record of fourteen assists, which he achieved in 1983–84, with Edmonton. Incredibly, he played only forty-five games that year. No other goalie has more than nine in a season (Curtis Joseph, in 1991–92, with St. Louis).

with six, and the only other goalie to offer any substantial offence was Henrik Lundqvist of the Rangers, who managed four. In 2009–10, the top goalie was Dallas's Marty Turco with four assists, and the year before it was Turco again, with five.

TOM BARRASSO.

GOALIE GOALS Of course, more spectacular than a goalie assist is a goalie goal, and this has been done only eleven times in NHL history. There are two kinds of goalie goals: one, where the goalie is credited with the goal because he was the last player to touch the puck before the other team puts it into its own net; and two, when a goalie shoots the puck into an empty net. No goalie has ever scored a goal against an opponent's goalie. Billy Smith of the Islanders got the first NHL goalie goal on November 28, 1979, an own goal by the Colorado Rockies on a delayed penalty.

Ron Hextall of the Flyers was the first to shoot the puck into the net for a goal, a feat he first accomplished on December 8, 1987. He did it again in the 1989 playoffs. Martin Brodeur also shot the puck in, regular season and playoffs, and Chris Osgood and Jose Theodore both scored goals as well. Damian Rhodes was credited with a goal, as were Mika Noronen and Chris Mason. Mason, was the last goalie to be credited with a goal, on April 15, 2006. Evgeni Nabokov, meanwhile, was the last to fire the puck in the net, on March 10, 2002.

RON HEXTALL.

NO PLAYER HAS TAKEN TWO SHOOTOUT SHOTS IN ONE GAME

THE RECORD Since the introduction of the shootout for the 2005–06 season, nearly 1,000 games have been decided by a shootout, but none lasted long enough for one player to take two shots in a game.

HOW IT WAS (NEVER) DONE The NHL rule for shootouts states that: "No player may shoot twice until everyone who is eligible has shot. If, however, because of injury or penalty, one team has fewer players eligible for the shootout than its opponent, both teams may select from among the players who have already shot. This procedure would continue until the team with fewer players has again used all eligible shooters." This rule has never been required as all shootouts have been decided within one round of the roster.

WHY IT WON'T BE EQUALLED The longest NHL shootout to date occurred on November 26, 2005. That night, thirty shots were taken; the final one, from Marek Malik of the Rangers, was the game winner against Washington. There were thirty-six skaters in the lineup (eighteen a side), but even still six more players would have to have shot before one could attempt a second time. Of course, the next NHL game could see a shootout go 100 rounds, but if it's never happened in 1,000 tries, it isn't likely to happen

THE RANGERS' MAREK MALIK ENDED THE NHL'S LONGEST SHOOTOUT.

UNBEATABLE GAME RECORDS

HOW MALIK BECAME A HERO

The Rangers and Capitals were tied 2–2 after regulation time and 5:00 of overtime, setting the stage for a shootout. Alexander Ovechkin went first for the Caps and was stopped by Henrik Lundqvist. Martin Straka missed as he came in on Caps' goalie Olaf Kolzig, and then teams exchanged goals, Andrew Cassels for the Blueshirts and Michael Nylander responding for Washington. Both Matt Pettinger (Washington) and Jaromir Jagr (Rangers) were stopped, and sudden death began. The next six shooters failed to tally, but Washington got the upper hand when Brian Willsie scored. Under pressure, Ville Nieminen responded for the Rangers. A drought of fourteen misses ensued, one shooter after another failing to hit the net or being stopped by the goalies. Bryan Muir eventually scored for the Caps, but he was matched by Jason Strudwick of the Rangers. Matt Bradley was stopped by Lundqvist and then Malik was called on for the Rangers. He hadn't scored all year and decided to do something fancy. Skating in on goal, he put his stick between his legs and flicked the puck from behind his body past a stunned Kolzig. Said teammate Jagr after the brave move: "You have to have guts to do that move. In front of 20,000 people watching you, it's not that easy to do." Perhaps not, but it ended the longest shootout in NHL history.

THE IIHF RECORD

International rules differ from NHL rules. In IIHF events, after each side takes three shots and the score is still tied, coaches can select any player he wants. In effect, he could choose the same player again and again, for the fourth shot, fifth shot, etc. Also, in international play, the order of shooting changes after three shots, so the team that went first for the first three rounds goes second for the fourth shot and on. And, in IIHF games, coaches can change a goalie after every shot if he wants. In the NHL, a goalie change can be made only in case of injury. Canada's Jonathan Toews set an IIHF record for most shootout goals when he scored three times in one U20 game, January 3, 2007, in the semi-finals against the United States.

tomorrow. Why? The format. Three shooters a side, most goals wins. The majority of shootouts are decided after these six shots. After that, it's sudden-death, each team getting one shot. The chances of going through the rest of the team's lineup so that a player is required to shoot a second time, are millions to one.

Malik's winner was notable for two reasons. One, he was a low-scoring defenceman who had just thirty-three career goals in thirteen seasons and 691 games. And two, despite his evident lack of scoring touch, he beat goalie Olaf Kolzig with one of the most daring shootout moves ever attempted, putting his stick between his legs and snapping the puck from behind his skates and in.

LONGEST SHOOTOUTS OUTSIDE NHL

The longest shootout in European hockey occurred on November 21, 2010, in Germany. The Straubing Tigers beat EHC Munchen, 5–4, after forty-two shots, each team taking twenty-one. The longest IIHF shootout took place on January 3, 2002, at the U20 in the Relegation Round. In a best-of-two series, both Belarus and France won one game each, forcing a shootout to decide which team stayed in the top division for 2003 and which team was demoted to Division I. The shootout went twenty-six shots (13 each), with Belarus finally winning. The longest shootout in women's hockey took place between Canada and the United States, in an exhibition game on October 12, 2003. A total of twenty-two shots were taken (11 a side) before the Americans won.

EDMONTON'S TAYLOR HALL BEATS ILYA BRYZGALOV WITH A SHOOTOUT GOAL.

ACKNOWLEDGEMENTS

THE AUTHOR WOULD LIKE TO THANK the many people who have supported the book and helped produce it, starting with M&S publisher Doug Pepper and Fenn/M&S publisher Jordan Fenn. As well, to the entire M&S production department for doing such a terrific job under some duress, notably editors Liz Kribs and Michael Melgaard, and designer Marijke Friesen, as well as Janine Laporte and Ruta Liormonas. As well, to my agent Dean Cooke and his team, including Mary Hu and Rachel Letofsky. To various people who abetted the research process, namely Julie Young at the NHL, Miragh Addis, Steve Poirier, and Darren Boyko at the Hockey Hall of Fame Resource Centre, and Szymon Szemberg and Kristina Koch at the IIHF. As well, thanks go to Craig Campbell and Phil Pritchard at HHOF, Paul Michinard at Getty, and Graig Abel. And lastly, to my own record-setting team off ice, especially Liz, Ian, Zach, and Emily, my mom and, lastly, wife, who has finally decided to settle down for a while, a record in itself never to be equaled.

PHOTO CREDITS

GETTY IMAGES pages 3, 5, 7, 10 (top), 11, 12, 14 (both), 15, 18, 22, 23, 24, 26, 27, 28, 30, 31, 32, 33, 34, 35, 38, 39, 41, 42, 43, 45, 46, 48, 49, 50, 51, 53, 54, 55, 56, 58, 62, 63, 64, 68, 70, 71, 72, 74, 75, 77, 78, 80, 81, 82, 83, 84, 87, 91 (both), 92, 95, 96, 97, 98, 99, 102, 104, 105, 107, 108, 109, 110, 111, 112, 113, 114, 115, 116, 117, 119, 123, 125, 126, 127, 128, 129, 130, 132, 133, 135, 136, 137, 140, 141, 144, 145, 146, 147, 148, 149, 152, 153, 158, 159, 160, 161, 164, 165, 166, 169, 170, 171, 172, 173, 174, 176, 182, 184, 185, 186, 190, 191, 192, 193, 194, 195, 196, 197, 200, 201, 202, 203, 204, 206

HOCKEY HALL OF FAME pages 19, 59, 89, 150, 180, 198

TUROFSKY COLLECTION/HOCKEY HALL OF FAME pages 65, 85, 154, 155, 162

GRAPHIC ARTISTS/HOCKEY HALL OF FAME pages 100, 103, 106

JUKKA RAUTIO—IIHF/HHOF IMAGES page 205

MILES NADAL/HOCKEY HALL OF FAME pages 142, 178

PAUL BERESWILL/HOCKEY HALL OF FAME pages 37, 127

IIHF ARCHIVES page 189

CP pages 4, 8, 10 (bottom), 76, 86, 94, 121, 124, 138, 156, 181

EDMONTON JOURNAL pages 40, 120

GRAIG ABEL page 168

BOSTON PUBLIC LIBRARY page 85

CITY OF MONTREAL ARCHIVES page 151